WHAT

"Dirk Helmling challenges Christians to recognize the disconnect that exists between what we say we believe and how we live our lives. Dirk has done a phenomenal job of providing a clear and concise plan to remedy this problem. Biblical discipleship must take center stage for every believer, every church, every pastor and every youth pastor around the world. If you and your church are even remotely interested in being faithful to the Great Commission, than *The Cost Of The Disconnect* is a must read for you! Dirk's book will be an invaluable resource for your library."

> **—JOSH McDOWELL,** *Josh McDowell Ministries*

"Dirk's book is a must read by everyone who desires to follow Jesus. Biblical discipleship has been misunderstood and patently ignored far too long. It's time the church takes seriously the call of Jesus to be and make disciples. *The Cost Of The Disconnect* will equip you and your church to do this with purpose and passion. Dirk's no-nonsense approach and style of writing puts the mandate from Scripture clearly on the table—be a disciple. Make disciples. Teach others to do the same. What an unmistakable and simple path to follow!"

> **—DR. BARRY ST. CLAIR,** *Executive Director, Reach Out Youth Solutions*

"Have you ever gotten too much horseradish up your nose? At first it burns, your eyes may even water, but the result can be very satisfying. *The Cost Of The Disconnect* is an olfactory shock that prepares you to enjoy even more horseradish with your prime rib, it makes it a tasty and a memorable experience. After the eye watering starts, because most of us feel uncomfortable with unadorned truth, I found reading Dirk's words very tasty. I hope his book wakes up the church. Yes he makes us squirm, but in the end, it could save many a leader from a life of misery, the life of wasting your time not being and making disciples."

> **—BILL HULL,** *Author of: Christlike, The Pursuit of Uncomplicated Obedience; Choose The Life; The Complete Book of Discipleship; Jesus Christ Disciple Maker*

"I know Dirk Helmling. I know his heart is bursting with a burden to see the truths of this book applied by pastors and true disciples of Christ. If every pastor and church planter was required and held accountable to apply the truths of Dirk's book, in the power of the Holy Spirit, we would see a revival that would be unprecedented in history."

> **—DR. STEPHEN D. HARRIS,** *Pastor of New Life Community Church, Asheville, North Carolina*

*The Cost Of The Disconnect*
by Dirk Helmling

Printed in the United States of America

ISBN 9781613792346

Front cover design: Dawson Helmling
Logo design: Dawson Helmling
Back cover design: 29.11 Ministries

www.xulonpress.com

# the Cost of the Disconnect

## the discipleship crisis and the global ramifications of an impotent church

### DIRK helmling

"Biblical discipleship must take center stage for every believer, every church, every pastor and every youth pastor around the world. Dirk has done a phenomenal job here...If you and your church are even remotely interested in being faithful to the Great Commission, than The Cost Of The Disconnect is a must read for you!"
—Josh McDowell, Josh McDowell Ministries

Xulon PRESS

# TO THE ONES I LOVE...

A wife of noble character is her husband's crown. My head is adorned with an invaluable treasure. Thank you, **Julie**, for being everything and more a guy could long for in a wife and partner in ministry. Has it really been eighteen years already? It seems like just yesterday we started this journey together at The Breakers in Palm Beach. You have become a Proverbs 31 woman and I pray our daughters grow up to be just like their mommy. Our journey together has been the ride of a lifetime and I can't wait to see what comes next. I love you!

**Dawson, Ezekiel, Cassie, Nana, Moses, Sydney, and Ephraim** - Your daddy cannot begin to imagine what life would be like without you here. Each day has been better than the last. You are indeed a heritage from the Lord and my prayer for each of you is that you would grow to love God more than you love anything and everything else. Thanks for being the best kids a guy could ever ask for. I love each of you to infinity and beyond.

**Mom** - Words fail me. How can I thank you for bringing me into this world? How can I say thanks for all the sacrifices you've made (and continue to make!) for me over the past forty years? As I grow in age, my love for you continues to deepen. It is a joy to know that we worship the same God and that we'll have all of eternity to tell Him how grateful we are for all that He is. Thanks for sticking around so we could celebrate this book together. I'll make you a deal — if you promise to hang around for #2, I promise I'll work fast. I love you, Mom!

**Jesus** - I am what I am and Your grace to me was not without affect. Rarely a day goes by that I don't think of where I'd be apart from You claiming me as Your own. I long to be satisfied with all that You are so that the remainder of my days will be spent making much of Your name among the nations. Your name and renown really are my innermost desires. Continue to enlarge my heart and I will run in the way of Your commands. I love You, Jesus!

# CONTENTS

7

# INTRODUCTION

Biblical discipleship is virtually obsolete from the vast majority of evangelical churches in North America. The radical and compelling call of Jesus to come and die has been replaced with a more palatable call of a Jesus imposter to come and claim your prizes.

It seems very few recognize the enormous disconnect between what the Bible clearly teaches about costly allegiance to Jesus and how we actually choose to live our lives. Most of us are quick to profess our adherence to base and fundamental Christian beliefs. Perhaps some of us might even readily acknowledge we are followers of Jesus. But when we navigate through the pages of Scripture and discover the mandates that Jesus places on His followers, it's difficult to overlook the giant disconnect that seems so pervasive among so many professing Christians. We claim Jesus with our lips but our lives tell a much different story. There most definitely exists a gargantuan disconnect between the call of Jesus and the response of many who profess to be His followers.

If we are indeed authentic disciples of Jesus Christ, we must take a thorough and painfully honest look at the cost of this disconnect. No doubt there is a high price to be paid for embracing an adulterated gospel that cherishes gift above Giver, health above sickness, comfort above suffering, receiving above giving, and excess above sacrifice. Distorting the gospel to accommodate the desires of our sinful and corrupt flesh does not happen without an enormous cost.

The message Jesus personally delivered to the world two thousand years ago was much different than the message we hear from many of our pulpits today. We want Jesus and all the benefits that we think come along with Him. But we're reluctant to embrace the heavy and costly requirements that Jesus places on those who decide to align themselves with Him.

If we detail the accounts of Jesus' interaction with potential proponents of His kingdom message, it's clear from Scripture that Jesus talked many people out of the kingdom. He was quick to remind potential adherents to consider the high cost of following Him before they signed on the dotted line. It was certainly indicative of Christ to wave the banner of warning in plain sight of would-be allies of His cross.

This then begs the question – If Jesus was so quick to warn people of the dangers of following Him, why don't we warn them as well? Why don't we let people know up front that their allegiance with Jesus might just cost them their lives? Why don't we caution people that in order to truly follow Jesus you need to be radically committed to obeying His Word? Why don't we give fair warning that becoming an ally of the cross will instantly put us at sharp odds with the world? Why don't we alert those who are contemplating following Jesus so they know up front that Jesus places significant demands on the lives of those who choose to embrace His radical message?[1]

The reason is simple. Because we've distorted the gospel so significantly that most see no threat or hazard with picking up their crosses and following Jesus. We've tamed Jesus to be nothing short of our heavenly genie who exists to make much of us instead of us existing to make much of Him. If Jesus offers a comfortable place to spend eternity and demands nothing of us while we remain here on earth, of course droves of people can and will embrace that proposition. And why wouldn't they? They've been taught the cost is inconsequential.

Radical followers of Jesus should feel compelled to expose the lie that is currently being systematically propagated across many of our churches in North America. A lie that teaches that radical discipleship is reserved for the spiritually elite and perhaps for those who are ready to make a commitment to get more serious about their faith. This heresy also teaches that Christianity is a system by which we get Jesus and all His many benefits while simultaneously being exempt from crushing pain and suffering. In other words, we've been conditioned to believe that aligning ourselves with Jesus ensures that our pleasures are maximized while our trials and hardships are minimized.

Much of American Christianity is a crock and a far cry from the message of the pure gospel. We must be tuned in to what Scripture teaches so we can refute anything and everything that reeks of this perverted gospel.

Together, let's journey through the pages of Scripture and explore the high cost of discipleship and the exorbitant cost of non-discipleship. As we'll discover, both have an incredibly significant price tag. And whether consciously or unconsciously, we've already made our decision and embraced one of these doctrines.

May God's kindness lead us to repentance if we become aware that we've embraced a form of the gospel that is void of the high cost of following Jesus. The stark reality is that much of the doctrine we hear being proclaimed from pulpits across our country is in fact non-discipleship Christianity, which as we'll discover, isn't Christianity at all.

I want to encourage you to take this journey with me. At times it might seem easier just to plead ignorance and pretend American Christianity isn't as bad as it really is. Other times it might seem compelling to abandon our mission altogether. Of course it would seem appealing at times to take the road most traveled. But please, resist the urge to do what comes easy. Don't compromise the truths of Scripture in an effort to temporarily satisfy the desires of your flesh. Purpose in your heart now to join those who willfully choose to follow Jesus, no matter what it costs them, no matter where it takes them, and no matter what sacrifices will need to be made along the way.

The cost of this disconnect is far too significant to ignore and the repercussions are too severe to overlook. We cannot simply walk away. Turning a blind eye is no longer an option. We must embrace the call of Jesus to come and die. In so doing we will gladly join our King as He sovereignly chooses to use us to take the gospel to the world and make disciples of all the nations.

I pray that God would help me waken in you a deep and unbridled desire to invest the remainder of your days being a passionate, Christ-exalting, God-honoring disciple of Jesus Christ who hears the clarion call to deliver the gospel and to make disciples in every village, in every city, on every island and on every square inch of land around the globe.

Join me as we run in the way of His commands to make His name great among the nations.


*For the sake of His name and renown,*


Dirk Helmling
December 2010

# A FRESH PERSPECTIVE

As I sit on the shore of the Sea of Galilee, I can't help but think of all the events that took place right here 2,000 years ago. The Sea isn't that big, so from the shore of where I sit I can see nearly the entire Sea. And it was here, right here from this very shoreline, that Jesus beckoned His first followers to walk away from the comforts and predictability of their lives in order to follow hard after Him.

I'm listening to Steven Curtis Chapman's song *For The Sake Of The Call*. I can't help but envision the scene when Jesus stepped into the lives of these ordinary fishermen. "Empty nets lying there at the water's edge told a story that few could believe and none could explain. How some crazy fishermen agreed to go where Jesus led, with no thought for what they would gain. For Jesus had called them by name. And they answered – 'We will abandon it all for the sake of the call.'"

Matthew (ch.4) records this story in detail as he writes:

> *"While walking by the Sea of Galilee, He saw two brothers, Simon and Andrew his brother, casting a net into the sea, for they were fishermen. And He said to them, 'Follow Me, and I will make you fishers of men.'"*

What an amazing statement that Jesus made to these men. Not a propositional promise. Not an if/then conditional promise. This was a clear and unmistakable promise of declaration. Simply put, Jesus told these men that as they chose to surrender their lives to follow hard after Him, He would radically change everything about them and give them something eternally significant to build their lives on.

Matthew goes on to record these life-changing events that would shape thousands of years of Biblical Christianity and would be the foundation of the very blueprint of Christ-centered discipleship. Matthew notes that immediately following Jesus' call, Simon and Andrew left their nets and followed Jesus. And as Jesus continued to walk down the shore of the sea from there, He saw two other brothers, James and John, in their boat with their dad Zebedee, mending their nets. Just like He had previously called Simon and Andrew, now He was beckoning James and John.

It's interesting and critical to note that Matthew's record of this event says that all four of these men dropped everything to follow Jesus. They left their family businesses, their families, their reputations, their comforts, their personal dreams and aspirations for their lives, etc. etc. And they did all of this knowing that this journey they were starting would not lead to fame. They chose to follow, simply because it was Jesus who was calling them.

It is early morning and as I write this on the shore of the Sea of Galilee, I can see six small fishing boats manned by the same type of simple men that Jesus called. And they have been busy toiling all night, looking for a great catch, just like the four men I mentioned earlier.

What was it about this Rabbi that compelled these men to walk away from everything that they knew in order to follow this man Jesus? What words did they hear roll off of His lips besides His simple invitation? What did they see? What did they see in Him besides a plain and ordinary man with a compelling call to live for something other than themselves?

16

Two thousand years later, Jesus is extending the same invitation to you and me. He has issued the call. The clarion call to lay down our lives and live for His cause. I can almost hear Him say *"Dirk, it's time. Lay down your dreams. Lay aside your past. Set aside all of your preconceived ideas of what you think I'm all about. I'm calling you to join Me as I make disciples of the world. I want you to invest everything that you are and everything that you have in becoming a radical disciple of Mine and making other disciples who will give the whole of their lives to My cause. Dirk, can I count on you? Are you in or should I look for someone else?"*

He is extending that same invitation to you, my friend. Jesus of Nazareth is calling you to lay down your nets so you can pick up His cross. Not for what you can get out of it, not because of some great promise of a better tomorrow, not for some dreamy assurance of a more secure future, not for applause or accolades. But simply because it is Jesus who is calling.

My prayer is that God will use this book and the pages you are about to read, to awaken in you a great desire to follow hard after the Master. That you would hear Him call you to invest the entirety of your life following hard after Him and making disciples of the nations. The call has been extended. The invitation has been delivered. The mandates have been made clear. Jesus is simply awaiting your reply.

I'm in. Are you? I will go. Will you?

*For the sake of His call,*

Dirk
March 6, 2011
Sea of Galilee

# A BARREN LANDSCAPE

## WHAT DO YOU SEE WHEN YOU LOOK AROUND

If you're meandering through a wildlife park on an African safari in Kenya, you'll no doubt see your share of elephants, lions, monkeys, zebras, water buffalo, hippos, and a host of other exotic animals.

And if you're making your way through the streets of London, England perhaps you'll see places like Buckingham Palace, Big Ben, Westminster Abby, London Bridge, The London Eye and Piccadilly Circus.

What if we took a journey together, not on an African safari or a double-decker red bus tour through the streets of London, but a journey through the sanctuaries and classrooms of evangelical churches across the landscape of America. What do you suppose we would find? What conclusions would we draw if we were able to take the pulse of Christianity amidst all the varied churches where Jesus is named?

Having been in church now for over two decades, I've been involved with both ends of the church spectrum - everything from mega churches to small, family chapels. Looking back, I'm grateful for all of those experiences. Truthfully, some were more enjoyable than others.

If you've been on a church staff before, then you know what it's like to witness way more of the church politics and behind the scenes junk than most would be comfortable seeing. Of course, the aim would be to learn as much as you can from all that stuff – whether the experiences were good or bad, right? At least that's been my goal. And I really do trust the Lord to continue to use everything He's led me through to mold and shape my heart and my vision for ministry so that I can clearly articulate to the body of Christ what a local, Acts 2 church should be marked by.

I've also spent the last eleven years speaking around the country. I'm blessed to have been afforded such amazing opportunities. Along the way I've met some great people and made some lifelong friends. Whether I was speaking to a group of 200 or 20,000 it's always been my desire that God would reveal His immense worth to those I was speaking to and that they would passionately and obediently respond to the gospel.

Having been to so many places and having met with such a wide variety of pastors, youth pastors, and church staffers across the country, I am increasingly convinced that the American church, by and large, is missing the mark in a specific and profoundly significant way. Not only are we missing the mark, but in essence we're ignoring clear, Biblical mandates while choosing to embrace a doctrine that is severely flawed. Somehow we've managed to embrace and propagate a version of the gospel and a philosophy of ministry that contradicts the very words and heartbeat of Jesus.

You don't have to be a theologian or a Bible scholar to see what I'm talking about. Next time you're in the local, Christian bookstore take a look at the titles of the books that make it to the prominent display tables and shelves. Open some of those books to the inside, back, jacket cover. This is typically where we read about the author - including where they serve, what organization or church they are a part of, where they live, how many kids they have, educational background, etc, etc. Have you ever noticed that one of the first things we are told about these authors is how many people are members of their church or organization? As if the larger the number, the more credibility the person has. Isn't it accurate to say that when we read these short bio's, we are often times impressed and enthralled by the apparent influence these people have? I'd be lying if I said I didn't used to be enamored by all those mesmerizing numbers and stats.

Please hear me - I'm not saying we shouldn't celebrate the work that God does in growing people, both individually and corporately. Of course we want to celebrate transformed lives. My concern lies with this subtle belief we have adopted that quietly boasts bigger is somehow better. The larger the numbers - whether conversion or membership, square footage or acreage - the more we conclude God's greatest blessings have landed on these churches. So, we look around and make our assessments of pastors and churches based on these simple jacket figures.

Let me try to explain what I'm talking about. Church A runs about 500 people. They have a huge AWANA program and

21

a kickin' UPWARD thing going on. Over the past two years they've seen tremendous numeric growth. So much so that they've recently started a capital campaign to raise 3.7 million dollars for their new facility. It'll more comfortably seat 700 people and have ample room for an additional 150 seats. Not to mention this new facility will have its own gymnasium, complete with workout station and kitchen facility, along with a state of the art media room.

Church B runs about 6,000 people. On Sunday mornings not only do they have the coolest worship team around town but they have a pretty hip and engaging senior pastor as well. He's incredibly articulate and by all accounts the best speaker in town on a given Sunday morning. It doesn't hurt that church B offers about 65 different ministries – something for everyone! If you drive a yellow car and like tomato sandwiches with extra mayo, they have a place for you. If you're divorced with children living at home, and struggle with OCD, they have a ministry tailored precisely to fit your particular needs. If you're looking for a Christian concert in the area, church B will deliver. With their state of the art facilities, they can host the biggest names in Christian music. They even have a bookstore/coffee house on the premises called, what else? Holy Grounds.

And then there's church C. Poor little church C. Their building appears a bit outdated and the grounds could use a little TLC. They don't have ample parking for all the cars that show up on a given Sunday. And their facilities? Well, let's just say their facilities look a bit disheveled and lack that certain curb appeal we're taught is necessary to reach all those "seekers" in the neighborhood. But, they've got a faithful young guy who consistently preaches the Word every Sunday. He doesn't water it down and he's obviously not just looking for some quick converts to inflate his numbers. He's clearly passionate about helping people understand Scripture. He has a genuine heart to come alongside those who are struggling in their relationship with God. It's clear from his preaching that his primary agenda is simply to bring glory to Jesus, whether by living or by dying. He makes no apologies as he faithfully delivers the unadulterated Word of Life each week. He doesn't drive a new car and doesn't have any starched shirts with the church logo embroidered on the chest pocket. He stays true to his personality and wears jeans and a t-shirt when he preaches.[1]

Church C doesn't have a really sweet decked out youth room though. As a matter of fact, all of the high school students spend Sunday mornings serving by teaching the elementary kids and hanging out with the senior adults.

When we look around and draw our conclusions and make our assessments, what criteria do we use to do our evaluating? Are we looking at facilities? Ministries offered? Budgets? Growth trends? Denominational affiliations?

Most of us have shopped for a church before. And whether consciously or unconsciously, we've looked at churches we've visited and determined, based on some pre-established criteria, which of the competing churches will someday earn our allegiance.

With that in mind then, perhaps it will resonate with you that what I've seen across the spiritual landscape of

American churches has been a bit disturbing. We live in a church culture that defines success by pragmatism, numeric growth, big buildings, moving worship "sets", the church's ability to meet our felt needs, power ties and tailored suits. And let's be honest – if a church is serving up some Starbucks coffee and a wide assortment of Krispy Kreme doughnuts, well then the search is over. The mothership has landed.

All joking aside, much of this is incredibly nauseating. My hunch is God is sickened and grieved by it as well. After all, He is the One who authored the words – "man looks at the outward appearance, but God looks at the heart."[2] God is also the One who said to the church at Laodicea that He would rather them be hot or cold, but because they were lukewarm, neither hot or cold, the indictment He pronounced on them was that He was about to spit them out of His mouth.[3]

None of this to say that all big churches are bad. Certainly not! There are many large, God-honoring, Christ-exalting churches out there - churches that happen to be large, but who are being faithful to the Word of God and producing radical followers of Jesus Christ. Although mega is a four letter word, it doesn't have to carry the stigma of a four letter word. Mega just means extremely large or mammoth.

If an extremely large church is fleshing out Acts 2, being faithful to Matthew 28, and the people have embraced their role of taking the gospel to the world as laid out in Romans 10 (all without getting sucked into the perverted American version of Christianity), then I applaud them. There aren't many mega churches who have embraced the radical call of a Savior who

24

demands that we live a sacrificial life for the sake of the gospel and for the sake of making His name great among the nations. But just for the argument, let's say there are a handful of mega churches across the landscape of America who have committed their resources to taking the gospel to the world and making disciples of all the nations. And they are doing it with great passion and enormous integrity. Their efforts should certainly be acknowledged.

But let's not pretend that there aren't also a plethora of mega churches littered across North America that bring shame and dishonor to the name of Christ. Week after week they allure the masses and put on a show that rivals anything Hollywood could ever produce. The crowds are appeased but the heart of God remains grieved.

For those of us who are committed to the authority of Scripture and who aim to make much of the glory of God, we must agree that most, if not all, of what impresses our flesh does not necessarily please the heart of God. Men may be awed by our ability to attract and grow large numbers, but God is unmoved. And we cannot get sucked into measuring our churches and the effectiveness of our ministries by the pragmatic standards of the world.

Encarta defines pragmatism like this: a straightforward practical way of thinking about things or dealing with problems, concerned with results rather than with theories and principles. And so we look around town, flip through the Christian yellow pages and make our decision. We determine that because church B is the biggest, fastest growing, and affords the most opportunities for our personal growth, it's obviously a natural fit and the church God most likely wants us to attend. That's pragmatism.

Most of us have seen the man dubbed "America's Smiling Pastor" a time or two before on TV. If you're naïve enough (no offense intended) to look at Joel Osteen's church and conclude that they must be doing something right, then you've swallowed the pragmatic pill. Let me clarify.

According to Osteen's website, they spent 95 million dollars to renovate the Compaq Center. Ninety five million dollars! Simply because Osteen found people willing to give nearly one tenth of a billion dollars to his capital campaign does not necessarily mean his ministry honors the Lord. Just because Osteen can pack an arena with 38,000 people every time the doors open, and just because he and his wife can put on *A Night of Hope* and fill stadiums with people willing to drop $23 to get in, does not mean God is being honored or that He is necessarily pleased. Nor does it mean they are doing anything of kingdom value. It just means, pragmatically speaking, what they are doing is working.

If their goal is to have a huge church or to speak to the masses, they've clearly figured out a way to do that and to do it effectively. However, if Joel and his staff are looking at producing radical disciples of Jesus Christ willing to follow hard after their Master and willing to walk away from the American Dream, well then, it would appear they have fallen miserably short. Simply put, Lakewood Church is failing at making Biblical disciples. How do I know that? Because I know Joel's mission and agenda is *not* to make radical, passionate, selfless followers of Jesus Christ. Go to Joel's website and read it for yourself.[4] And I quote "Joel's extraordinary success can be found in his core message: That our God is a good God who desires to bless those who are obedient and faithful to Him through Jesus Christ. It is Joel's deepest desire that his own life be an example of that principle and that everyone who hears this message of hope and encouragement would choose to accept God's goodness and mercy and to become all that God wants them to be." End quote.

Where does this message come from? Certainly this is not the central message and theme of the Bible, is it? Have I overlooked something? Is there a piece of pivotal core doctrine that I've been ignoring? This Bible I'm reading fleshes out much differently than that. I once heard Joel say that because of God's favor on him that day, he was able to score a desirable, front row parking place at Wal-Mart. (Just thinking – if I get the front row parking place, doesn't that mean someone else doesn't?)

Really? Is Joel being serious when he makes comments like this? Of course he's being serious. He is genuinely sincere. He's got a million dollar smile that would make a toothpaste model envious. He's a likeable guy. Throw his gorgeous wife Victoria in the mix and you've got the likes of a Hollywood Power Couple. And you can't argue with the fact that they are indeed a Power Couple. They've sold millions of books (every title has the words Me, You, or Your in it).[5] They preach to a live crowd of nearly 38,000 people each week. Joel's sermons are viewed in over 100 countries and an estimated 20 million Americans tune in each month to watch.

Arguably, if we're simply looking at this pragmatically, Joel has arrived. He's hitting a home run every week. Not just a home run at the local baseball park, but a grand slam in the perverted arena of American Christianity and the saturated grandstands of Christian consumerism. If the gauge by which we're measuring "success" is bigger and better, than by all accounts Joel and Victoria Osteen and Lakewood Church have certainly arrived. And they didn't sneak in the back door either. They showed up in a stretch limo and are unapologetically walking the red carpet of American, showboat Christianity.

But, if we're measuring "success" by Biblical standards, and if we're looking at the life and message of Jesus, then our assessment would be very much different. (We're going to talk much more in depth about the message of Jesus and our response to it in future chapters. For now though we're just taking a look at the landscape around us and trying to assess what we find.)

Perhaps you think using Joel Osteen as an example of pragmatism is mean and wrong, because it just isn't kind. If that's seriously what you're thinking right now, perhaps this book isn't for you. Because the truth is, it gets worse. I'm really not trying to single out Joel and his church. I'm simply holding up his extremely popular model of American Christianity and comparing it to the model and message Jesus gave us throughout the gospels and the New Testament epistles.

If you think using Joel as an example isn't a good idea because Lakewood Church is not indicative of the average church in America, you've got a point. Although there are very few churches in America that match Lakewood in size and stature, certainly there are an abundance of churches littered across America that are strategically following the Lakewood Church model very closely. And most pray that the same spirit of blessing and anointing would in like manner fall on their church as well.

If you remember, Paul left Timothy in Ephesus to take care of some church matters. One of which was defending truth against false teachers. Paul said "Certain persons, by swerving from these, have wandered away into vain discussion, desiring to be teachers of the law, without understanding either what they are saying or the things about which they make confident assertions."[6] It would seem obvious that the aforementioned false teachers and content of their message to those unsuspecting listeners in Ephesus would closely parallel many of the false teachers filling our pulpits today.

It's difficult for me to think that nice, well dressed, articulate, passionate people can be false teachers. But Scripture is clear. These carnivorous beasts do not come dressed as the Big, Bad Wolf. If they were that obvious, they would not appear to be sheep. They would appear to be wolves. But, God's Word makes it abundantly clear that there are indeed men and women who dress like sheep, sound like sheep, eat like sheep, and hang out with other sheep, but who are in fact savage in their intentions and equally savage in their appetites. And we are exhorted to be on guard and watch out for them.

Let's consider an entirely different church paradigm - Willow Creek Community Church in South Barrington, Illinois. For many years they were arguably the church model that thousands of other churches around the world were looking at and desiring to emulate. And to some degree, they still are. WCCC was a program driven church for several decades and proudly boasted their program based model was worth emulating. They were not shy in declaring their church model was the pattern to follow if you wanted to grow an influential church with global status.

We now know Bill Hybels, pastor of Willow Creek Community Church, has had a dramatic change in perspective. His paradigm has shifted substantially. There's much more to the story, but here's an excerpt from an article about Bill Hybels and WCCC.

"Few would disagree that Willow Creek Community Church has been one of the most influential churches in America over the last thirty years. Willow, through its association, has promoted a vision of church that is big, programmatic, and comprehensive. This vision has been heavily influenced by the methods of secular business. James Twitchell, in his new book *Shopping for God*, reports that outside Bill Hybels' office hangs a poster that says: "What is our business? Who is our customer? What does the customer consider value?" Directly or indirectly, this philosophy of ministry - church should be a big box with programs for people at every level of spiritual maturity to consume and engage - has impacted nearly every evangelical church in the country.

So what happens when leaders of Willow Creek stand up and say, "We made a mistake"?

Not long ago Willow released its findings from a multiple year qualitative study of its ministry. Basically, they wanted to know what programs and activities of the church were actually helping people mature spiritually and which were not. The results were published in a book, *Reveal: Where Are You?*, co-authored by Greg Hawkins, executive pastor of Willow Creek. Hybels called the findings "earth shaking," "ground breaking," and "mind blowing."

Hawkins says, "Participation is a big deal. We believe the more people participating in these sets of activities, with higher levels of frequency, will produce disciples of Christ." This has been Willow's philosophy of ministry in a nutshell. The church creates programs/activities. People participate in these activities. The outcome is spiritual maturity. In a moment of stinging honesty Hawkins says, "I know it might sound crazy but that's how we do it in churches. We measure levels of participation."

Having put so many of their eggs into the program-driven church basket, you can understand their shock when the research revealed that, "Increasing levels of participation in these sets of activities does *not* predict whether someone's becoming more of a disciple of Christ. It does *not* predict whether they love God more or they love people more."

Speaking at the Leadership Summit, Hybels summarized the findings this way:

> "Some of the stuff that we have put millions of dollars into thinking it would really help our people grow and develop spiritually, when the data actually came back, it wasn't helping people that much. Other things that we didn't put that much money into and didn't put much staff against is stuff our people are crying out for."

Having spent thirty years creating and promoting a multi-million dollar organization driven by programs and measuring participation, and convincing other church leaders to do the same, you can see why Hybels called this research "the wake-up call" of his adult life.

Hybels confesses:

> "We made a mistake. What we should have done when people crossed the line of faith and become Christians, we should have started telling people and teaching people that they have to take responsibility to become 'self-feeders.' We should have gotten people, taught people, how to read their Bible between service, how to do the spiritual practices much more aggressively on their own."

In other words, spiritual growth doesn't happen best by becoming dependent on elaborate church programs but through the age old spiritual practices of prayer, Bible reading, and relationships. And, ironically, these basic disciplines do not require multi-million dollar facilities and hundreds of staff to manage.

Does this mark the end of Willow's thirty years of influence over the American church? Not according to Hawkins:

> "Our dream is that we fundamentally change the way we do church. That we take out a clean sheet of paper and we rethink all of our old assumptions. Replace it with new insights. Insights that are informed by research and rooted in Scripture. Our dream is really to discover what God is doing and how He's asking us to transform this planet.""[7]

I'm sure you'll agree that Willow should be applauded for their willingness to stop long enough to ask the hard questions, listen for the answers, and then make the necessary changes so that their efforts more clearly line up with the heart and will of God. And while I'm genuinely grateful that Bill was honest enough to publicly confess their mistakes and the unbiblical paradigm they held for so long, I'm not sure I would draw the same conclusions as he did.

Bill's conclusion, in part, was that they should have helped people take responsibility to become "self-feeders". While I certainly agree with this in part, I want to make sure you understand this book is devoted to the call of Jesus on our lives to *be* and *make* disciples. And as you'll discover, disciples are not self-feeders. At least not initially.

Of course, at some point in time, people absolutely do need to take ownership for their own faith and can't always be led around like a new puppy or a toddler. However, at the core of radical, Biblical discipleship is a model that hinges on having someone else (rabbi/teacher) teaching you (student). It's not so much a 'self-feed' as it is a teacher/student paradigm. Certainly disciples are expected to grow to the level of maturity where they are much more capable of sitting at the feet of the Master Teacher Himself and feasting from His direct teaching and influence. But until that ability and discipline is achieved, disciples are far more dependent on the teacher/student paradigm. Much more on this in later chapters.

While Lakewood and Willow Creek are two incredibly large churches, it is no secret they are two very powerful models that pastors and youth pastors alike are holding up and feverishly trying to emulate. The truth is, even if we removed these powerhouse church models from the church landscape today, the average church in America is still woefully misaligned and missing the most fundamental and key component of Biblical Christianity, namely radical discipleship.

My observations are simple – we are not making disciples who are able to make other disciples. It simply is not happening. I know, I know, there are some churches out there doing it right. And I would love to hold those guys up as models for the rest of us to follow. They get it. They understand the difference between American Christianity and Biblical Christianity. And they are not willing to sacrifice clear Biblical mandates in order to have the fastest growing youth group or church in town. Kudos to these men and women!

While there certainly are pockets of guys scattered around the country whose aim it is to make God-honoring, Christ-exalting, radical, passionate disciples of Jesus Christ, this begs the question - what are the rest of us doing? If we're not making radical disciples, then what exactly are we doing? How are we measuring growth? What standard do we use to determine whether what we're doing is working or not? Are we holding up a pragmatic, me-centered standard to assess and evaluate our ministries or are we holding up the Word of God and assessing the effectiveness of our ministries based on Biblical principles and mandates? My hunch is our standard of evaluating what's happening in and around our ministries is not the same standard of measurement that God uses throughout the pages of Scripture.

Allow me to share a few quick examples. I see a lot of church staffers working incredibly long hours. Just this week I talked with a youth pastor that said he hadn't had an extra day off for nearly five months. Five months! So I'm certainly not arguing that our pastors need to work longer hours. As a matter of fact, I think they should work less hours and spend more time with their families. It's no secret that PK's and MK's don't have the greatest track records. Research shows that children who have parents in the ministry more often than not grow up to become thoroughly disengaged from traditional Christianity and wholly disconnected from whatever faith they may have claimed in their younger days.

Do we ever pause long enough to ask ourselves why this happens at such alarming rates? Much of it can be traced back to the pastor's noble and applauded efforts to save the world. But while we're off trying to rescue the world (all the while being applauded and esteemed by everyone for doing it), we often forfeit our most basic and fundamental ministry of making disciples in our own homes. And the fruit from our absence and neglect is painfully obvious. We indeed reap what we sow.

Even with these apparent discrepancies and obvious repercussions, the people in our churches continue to expect us to work sixty hours a week, be at every wedding and every funeral, make all the hospital rounds, plan all the retreats and camps, oversee staff development and training, etc, etc. Meanwhile, our wives and kids are home wondering where daddy is. It seems that over the years we've been conditioned to believe that it's okay to abandon our families because we're doing "ministry". It's way past the time for those of us holding ministry positions to take a bold stand and declare: *"I will no longer sacrifice my family on the altar of ministry. My first ministry is in my home."*

Just yesterday I spoke with a good friend of mine in Florida who is on staff at a church of about 350. The senior pastor is in his mid-fifties with no kids at home and takes home a comfortable 90,000 bucks a year. My friend, on the other hand, is in his mid-thirties. His total package is just a few thousand dollars over the poverty level. He's married with several small children at home. He qualifies for food stamps and government assistance. And he recently discovered the church is piling more onto his already overloaded job description.

It seems our churches are filled with a plethora of programs and activities. Many of us are running two and three services on any given Sunday. Some even have a Saturday night service to help accommodate more folks and cater to the growing number of people looking for an alternative to traditional church. And many churches around the country host a community service with other churches in their area. Most would admit though that Sunday school attendance hasn't seen measurable growth for decades and we're just barely holding our own for the majority of our Wednesday night activities.

Do we stop long enough to ask ourselves what in the world we're doing with all that we've been given? Are we even trying to ascertain whether or not we're investing in the things that God has mandated us to spend our time and resources on? Isn't it true that many of us get so caught up in the hustle and bustle of church activities and busy calendars that we rarely schedule the necessary time to intentionally recalibrate, readjust, and realign our lives and ministries? I hope it goes without saying that these times of introspection and assessment are vital and critical to having healthy lives and God-honoring ministries.

My twelve year old son visited a friend's church several years ago, which just happened to be the Sunday before Christmas. He came home with a bag full of candy and white "snow" in his hair. He was excited to tell me they had artificial snow blowing all over the place – "enough snow to fill our dining room and kitchen up to my waist!" he shouted. I asked him what he learned that night. He looked at me a bit puzzled. I clarified by asking, "What did Jason talk about, Dawson? What passage did he use?" To my dismay, my son said, "Dad, we didn't talk about the Bible at all, we just played games." While this may not be a typical representation of what this particular church normally does, it is certainly an accurate portrait of what has become ordinary for so many churches and youth groups around our country.

Why am I sharing these stories? What do they have to do with Biblical discipleship? Glad you asked. They have everything to do with Biblical discipleship. God-honoring, Christ-exalting, radical, Biblical discipleship has at its core, an unwavering commitment to obeying Biblical principles. And it's virtually impossible to be unapologetically committed to the process of making disciples by teaching folks how to obey Biblical principles, when our senior pastors, elders, and church leadership teams are not themselves entirely committed to radical, costly obedience.

Here's where the rubber meets the road. Remember the youth pastor I told you about who hadn't had an extra day off for five months? I don't know the leadership team at his church but they should be insisting that their pastors take the necessary time off to rest their bodies, their hearts, and their minds. Ministry can be incredibly taxing. That's why the burn out rate is so high among those in full-time ministry. This is precisely why we need more under-shepherds who are keeping a close watch on those who serve alongside of them. And pastors and leaders must be continually reminded that none of us are indispensable. When we fully embrace that truth, it removes much of the sense of urgency that dominates our thinking and causes us to be habitually busy doing good things at the expense of doing the best things.

Remember the story of the artificial snow my son told me about? Well, I'm not advocating we all become stoic nor am I saying that our meeting times can't include some laughs and good times. What I am contending though is that we must be vigilant in our efforts to ensure the Word of God is held in proper esteem. It must be the central component of everything that we do. Our activities and our strategies must flow from a clear understanding of Scripture and firm convictions birthed out of our time in God's Word.

Students should not mistake radical discipleship with fun and games. When we offer amusements and attractions to lure people in, we must continually offer fun and games to keep them in. Do we really need to be reminded that the authority of God's Word must be the impetus of everything we do in ministry? My fear is that somewhere along the way, the Word of God has taken a very prominent place....not just on stage left or on the back row, but in a storage closet in the basement. That's certainly not to say we shouldn't play games and have fun. I'm simply saying that if you choose to spend time doing those things, it should be painfully aware that they are the peripheral and a distant second to teaching God's Word and making disciples of those in your care.

My friend that I told you about (who's making one third of what his boss is making) should get a raise. And I'm certainly not saying that because he's my friend. I'm saying this because there is simply no way to justify one guy making three times what another guy makes – ON A CHURCH STAFF! That completely contradicts the model and the heart of the message we find in Acts 2.

This kind of disproportionate compensation is widely embraced and accepted in the corporate world where unregenerate CEO's do not follow Biblical principles. And sadly it's a practice that is widely accepted in the church as well. But of all places, our churches should be the laboratory where we flesh out the truths we find in Scripture. And you simply cannot justify two full-time guys being on the same church staff with such vast discrepancies in their wages. Fair for the world? Perhaps. Acceptable in the church? Absolutely not!

Pastors and Youth Pastors - We have such a limited amount of time to invest in our people each week. Why do we continue wasting our time playing silly games and offering up irrelevant devotions aimed only at meeting the superficial needs of our flock? Have we really reduced God to this? Don't we have a high calling to deliver the Word of God each time we have the opportunity? And haven't we been commissioned to do much more than just place band-aids on severed limbs?

Let's remind ourselves that the Word of God is powerful and effective, sharper than any two edged sword. It's able to penetrate deep into the hearts of those in our midst. We've been given such a relatively short amount of time to invest in these lives, let's make the most of it. Let's purpose to raise the bar, offer more, expect more, risk more, all in an effort to make His name great among the nations.

Students and Adults – We too have a very small amount of time to invest each week. Why do we settle for plastic trinkets and cold leftovers while the King of the universe is beckoning us to lose our lives in our pursuit of following hard after Jesus? His call is too compelling and His proposition to us is far too significant to waste any more time settling for cheap imitations.

We would do well to recognize that Jesus demands more of our lives than mere attendance and simple participation with the status quo. If that is the entirety of what your leaders are offering and expecting of you and your family, let me encourage you to find another church.

How can we invest money on advertising, prizes, games and food, pack a room full of students (or adults!) on any given Sunday or Wednesday of the year, and not crack open our Bibles? How is it possible to throw away two hours playing mindless games and devouring truckloads of sugar and yet not carve out some strategic time to address the dire spiritual needs of the sheep God has entrusted to us? How can we encourage our members to show up on any given night of the week without helping them feast on the very words of life? What does it say about our own doctrine when we have a room full of students and adults and we spend more time talking about sports and the weather, then we spend talking about what it means to respond to the radical call of Jesus to abandon our lives for the sake of the gospel?

Maybe we're not convinced the spiritual needs around us are as significant as they really are and that Jesus wasn't serious when He called us to abandon all for the sake of His name and renown. Or it could be that we've just been duped into thinking it's our job to make church activities attractive so people will keep showing up.

I'm really not trying to be hyper critical about the church. Honest, I'm not. But as I look around and assess what's going on in many of our churches today, I always come back to the same question - *are we producing radical, passionate, selfless disciples of Jesus Christ?* Are we being intentional about helping people to understand clearly the radical call of Jesus to lay down our lives and follow hard after Him? Are we painting a clear picture of what it means to be identified with Jesus? Do we exist to spread amongst our people a passion for the supremacy of God? Are we rallying together a remnant of Christ followers who will join the prophet Isaiah in saying "Yes, Lord, walking in the way of Your laws, we wait for You; Your name and renown are the desire of our hearts."?[8] Are we helping our people develop a God-centered, Christ-exalting, Bible-saturated passion for their lives that's worth living for and worth dying for? Do our people have any concept of the magnitude of the sovereignty of God and how crucial that understanding is in order to properly assess and respond to so much of the pain, suffering, and despair that we see around us? Do *we* have a Biblical concept of the magnitude of God's sovereignty?

It seems many are confusing our God given purpose and mandate to make disciples with growing a bigger and more prominent church. Have we knowingly or unknowingly equated our busy church calendars with adherence to Biblical commands? Is it possible that we've set aside the hard job of tending the soil, making radical disciples of Jesus in exchange for an easier, more manageable agenda where the "success" rates are seemingly much higher? As much as it pains me to say this, I'm certain far more than not have caved in to American Christianity, embraced a false gospel, and are marketing a bogus bill of goods to millions around the world.

One of my first church staff experiences was in a small town in the Eastern part of the country. My wife and I had just moved to the area and not long after we got settled a local church called and asked me if I'd consider talking with them about being their youth pastor. I was already employed at a high end country club in town - a second home community, complete with a golf course and private landing strip, all atop a 3,600 foot mountain. This unique development offered gorgeous, multi-million dollar estates with outrageous views across the Blue Ridge Mountains.

My wife and I were both working there and I had just been offered an amazing, once in a lifetime opportunity. A sales position was vacant. I had my real estate license and was primed for the job. I could have earned a conservative $200,000 my first year selling. That's pretty comical because my previous five years of income combined wouldn't have totaled $200,000. Needless to say, I was initially intrigued and interested.

Timing was everything. God was setting this whole thing up to ensure I would not compromise my loyalties and commitment to the cause of Christ. Would I jump on the chance to make an astronomical amount of money that would temporarily satisfy the cravings of my flesh? Or would I take a position at an obscure little church with a meager little salary and continue to exhaust my life and limited resources making disciples?

You've probably figured out by now that I chose the church job. Not because I had a black belt in Christianity, but because I knew I could not have been faithful and committed to the mandate of making disciples while selling real estate and working 80 hour weeks.

Truth be told, I wrestled with this decision for more than just a few minutes. My wheels were spinning like crazy. The thought of bringing home that much money was simply mind blowing to me. I found myself daydreaming about all the cool things we could do with such a cushioned bank account. And of course I was simultaneously contemplating ways to invest part of it in the kingdom. After all, I couldn't have justified it without entertaining ideas of how we could spend at least part of it on something other than ourselves. Pretty noble of me, huh? But at the end of the day I knew it just wouldn't work. It couldn't work. I would not have been satisfied with $200,000. Initially it would have been great. But at some point our standard of living would have increased and I would have wanted more. All the while God's mandate to invest my life making disciples would have been ignored and my heart would have been seared.

Unfortunately though, for the small church I mentioned above, discipleship was not high on their list of priorities. As a matter of fact, they didn't even know what Biblical discipleship was. They had mistakenly assumed that because they had two Sunday services and a myriad of men's and women's groups that met together that they were somehow fulfilling Jesus' clear mandate to make disciples.

I remember a few of the high school guys at this church that I introduced to radical, Biblical discipleship. They really had no concept that there was anything other than your average 'youth group' meeting on Sunday nights. For some, that exposure to Biblical discipleship wrecked their lives and they are now wasting their lives on the kingdom because of that investment. Micah, I'm proud of you!

Many years later I joined the staff of another church in the same part of the country. They had a likable, articulate senior pastor and boasted the largest mission's budget amongst Baptist churches throughout this state. To my knowledge, when I joined the staff none of the other pastors or elders were regularly discipling anyone. Dreadfully sad but painfully true.

The church organized and promoted domestic and international mission trips throughout the year and even had a significant investment in an unreached people group. The church had a special budget for indigent people and often times even paid the bills for local families who were unable to financially cover their own utilities. By most accounts the church was vibrant and healthy. Unless of course, the standard of assessment was the intentionality of helping people become radical, Biblical disciples who would reproduce themselves by making other disciples.

The most recent church staff I was a part of was a friendly church in the Midwest. And again unfortunately, to my knowledge, none of the other pastors and only one of the eight elders, besides myself, were discipling anyone. In essence, the leadership had not taken seriously the Great Commission and could not then encourage their people to commit the whole of their lives to being and making radical, Biblical disciples. They had apparently not found this God-centered, Christ-exalting, Bible-saturated, kingdom task worth giving the whole of their lives for.

Needless to say, this description is not unique or odd. It's happening in thousands of churches around our country, even now. And it's increasingly becoming the norm.

How did we get so far off course? Where did we go wrong? How can thousands of churches across the landscape of America wave the banner of Christianity while missing the very core of what Biblical Christianity is about? At what point did we abandon the mandate handed down for twenty centuries to be and make Biblical, radical, selfless, passionate, zealous disciples of Jesus Christ?

My observations of the current discipleship vacuum and the convictions that God has placed in my own heart about this are the primary factors that have given rise to this book. I certainly don't claim to have all the answers. Even with sixteen or eighteen books in my library about discipleship, I still do not claim to have the answers. Well, I'm not claiming to have *all* of the answers anyway.

My efforts contained in this book are simply to expose the discipleship crisis that currently exists today and to help all of us see how radically different our church paradigm is from the paradigm that Jesus created, promoted, and launched during His ministry. We can no longer deny the global ramifications of the non-discipleship version of Christianity we've embraced for so long. It is indeed high time we sound the alarm and wave the banner so the church of Jesus Christ gets serious about what Jesus Christ Himself is serious about.

I am incredibly burdened that so many pastors, youth pastors, church staffers, elders, and leaders are proclaiming a fractured and adulterated gospel. We talk a lot about God and Jesus and all the benefits of heaven, but are we really proclaiming the hard truths of Scripture and teaching people about the supremacy and sovereignty of God? Are we modeling a lifestyle of sacrifice and obedience, love and forgiveness, humility and selflessness, or are we selling a warped gospel in which God exists to make much of us and whose primary agenda is to make us healthy and wealthy? Have we compromised the gospel and deluded ourselves into thinking Jesus left the glory of heaven to make His way to planet earth simply to make much of us? It's painfully clear that many of us have indeed embraced this attractive yet horribly skewed doctrine.

Doesn't it seem like the primary goal in many of our churches today is simply to get as many people as possible to pray the "sinner's prayer"? But in order to do that, we've eliminated the central, costly message of the gospel. Namely that Jesus is calling us to band together as His radical followers, obey His Word, and make much of His name among the nations, even when that costs us our lives. Haven't we in essence simplified the gospel to be little short of a fast pass to heaven and our 'get out of jail free' card from hell?

Remember the old illustration of the frog in the kettle? In the early 90's George Barna even wrote a book with that title. Perhaps some of you have read it. The premise is this - If you put a frog in a kettle of water and over the course of much time, slowly turn up the heat, the frog will be completely and utterly oblivious of his impending death. The frog's environment changes so slowly that he doesn't even know he's about to be boiled to death.

Aren't we much like the frog in the kettle? We've been placed smack dab in the center of what has been coined American Christianity. Little by little and very slowly over the course of time, we become increasingly oblivious to the compromises and subtle discrepancies between Biblical Christianity and American Christianity.

Among other things, secularism, materialism, pluralism, and pragmatism have all played a crucial role in the church's dire and critical state of affairs. Before many of us even become aware of what's happening around us, we're already completely submerged in a church culture that carries a Christian title but has little resemblance to the radical message Jesus introduced to the world two thousand years ago.

It's high time we plead with God to remove us from the kettle of American Christianity and establish our hearts and our ministries firmly on the foundational truths of Scripture. The time has come for us to reject easy-believism and cheap grace in order to embrace the radical, costly message of Biblical allegiance found in the pages of God's Word.

## OUR PRAYER

*Lord Jesus, You are the only One worthy of our attention and our affection. You alone stand as Ruler and King over everything. We confess to You that our hearts have wandered and we've embraced a fractured and broken gospel. We acknowledge that any doctrine that we adhere to that minimizes the high cost of following You pales in comparison to the liberating truth we find in the pages of Scripture. As we begin to contemplate the high cost of following hard after You, we long for our hearts to resonate with the apostle Paul in saying 'to live is Christ and to die is gain.'*

*We echo the words of Isaiah when we say 'walking in the way of Your truth, we wait for You. Your name and renown are the desire of our hearts.' We confess that we are not as desperate for You as we should be. Wean us from our appetite for the crumbs of the world and teach us to hunger and thirst for the words of life that You offer those who follow hard after You.*

*Thank You, Father, for being patient towards us. We bless You and we recognize that Your mercies are new every morning. We are alive today because You continue to cause our hearts to beat. Teach us to number our days that we may gain a heart of wisdom. Make us aware of Your presence in the world and teach us to hear Your voice and respond obediently. Change our hearts and use us to make Your name great among the nations.*

*For the glory of Your name we pray. Amen.*

# THE CYCLE OF INSANITY
## AS A DOG RETURNS TO HIS VOMIT

The classic definition of insanity is: doing the same thing over and over again expecting different results. We've all been insane at times. Okay, well maybe not literally, but certainly we've all made decisions that appear insane. We've done things the same ol' way, hoping for and anticipating a much different outcome.

I usually explain it like this. If you have an equation (A+B+C=D), then no matter how you add up the A, B, and C, it will *always* equal D. Whether you add C plus B plus A, or B plus A plus C, the net result will always be D. Now, if you're good with D then this doesn't really pose any particular problem. However, if you don't like D and you're looking for something a little closer to E or M, well then you have a bit of a quandary on your hands. You can't keep using the same formula (A+B+C) because invariably, you will not get E or M. Predictably, you will continue to get D.

We know this. Most of us understand the basic components of a simple mathematic equation like the one above. For whatever reasons though, we don't readily see how the foundational principles of this basic math formula translates into our spiritual lives.

Pertaining to our spiritual lives, most of us would quickly confess we are painfully aware that something is missing. We know when we read Scripture we discover the details of how men and women who were following Jesus had something we often find void in our own pursuit of Jesus. Their lives were marked by a sense of desperation, urgency, and radical obedience we have not yet discovered and embraced for ourselves.

John records a story of Jesus interacting with some of His followers. His words were difficult to embrace and seemed impossible to adhere to. Jesus' terms for following Him were so weighty, in fact, that many of His disciples turned back and no longer walked with Him. They just couldn't justify losing their lives in order to save their lives. And when Jesus turned to the twelve and asked them if they were going to leave Him as well, Simon Peter responded by saying "Lord, to whom shall we go? You have the words of eternal life, and we have believed, and have come to know, that You are the Holy One of God."[1]

Have we gotten to the place where we are willing, better yet compelled, to join Peter in saying "Lord Jesus, You have the words of eternal life, and I have believed and have come to know, that You are the Holy One of God."? Are we able to see the net results of our own spiritual exercises up to this point have not produced the kind of radical, God-honoring, Christ-exalting lives we were designed and called to live?

Even though I might be able to articulate my spiritual misery or quandary, if I don't do anything to change it, I am most likely not that dissatisfied and apparently not convicted of the nasty sin of complacency and mediocrity that looms in the depths of my heart. The principle in place here is this – desperate people do desperate things. When a crack junkie is in need of his next hit or a pot smoker is jonesing for her next high, they will undoubtedly go to great lengths to ensure they are able to get what they feel like they need. If you know an addict or are a former addict yourself, you know what desperate measures people are willing to take to get that insatiable fix.

Just last week my cousin told me that she once sold a $15,000 Honda Accord for three small crack rocks. Her willingness to trade a car to get a temporary fix shows a profound level of desperation most of us have never personally experienced.

I was talking with a friend recently who told me his cousin was at the hospital visiting his dad who had just had major surgery. His dad had a bottle of Vicodin sitting on his tray table. This guy actually took his dad's pills in a futile effort to satisfy his own cravings. He was desperate. Desperate enough to steal from his own dad. Unfortunately for him, those twenty pills cost him his life. Remember, desperate people do desperate things.

This reminds me of Paul's description of some of the people in Corinth that he mentioned in 2 Corinthians 4.4 'The god of this age has blinded the minds of unbelievers, so that they cannot see the light of the gospel that displays the glory of Christ, who is the image of God.'

Do you see the similarities? Satan is obviously blinding the minds of unbelievers from seeing the reality of their dire situations. Satan is indeed the father of lies and it is his aim to steal, kill, and destroy. I am reminded though that Satan can only do what is sovereignly permitted by the Father. Satan's leash is only as long as God allows it to be. He wreaks havoc on the world every minute of every day. But the havoc he wreaks on this world does not fall outside the scope of God's supremacy and His sovereignty. God allows only that which He will use to make much of the glory of Jesus. I commend to you John Piper's book *Spectacular Sins* for a thorough discussion of how sin fits into the global, redemptive, sovereign purposes of God.

Aren't we all a bit insane at times? Spiritually speaking I mean. It's true. Listen. Don't we dream of a closer walk with God? Don't we imagine ways to have a profound, global impact on the world? Haven't there been times when we've confessed our sins to God, pouring out our honest and repentant hearts before Him, promising that we will not fall into the same sin we've been guilty of so many times prior? And often times we're deluded into thinking that somehow things are going to change, even though we're not adding anything different to the mix. At times, aren't we all deceived and blinded, at least to some degree, by the god of this age?

We must be cognoscente of the fact that if we continue to repeat the same behavior, without adding anything new to the mix, we can expect the same predictable outcome. And as we take a look at the spiritual landscape across our country, these same general principles can be applied.

The harsh reality is that if we don't make some drastic changes to the equation, we will continue to get the same results. What are those results? Well, it would be safe to say that the American church in the Western world, by and large, is not effective in making radical, God-honoring, Christ-exalting, Biblically literate, reproducing disciples of Jesus Christ. We may do a lot of things well, but when it comes to assessing our faithfulness to the mandate in Matthew 28, we must conclude that we've failed. And we've failed miserably.

Check out the information below and on the following page. If you weren't already convinced there is a giant chasm between what we think we're teaching from our pulpits and what our people are actually learning, I trust the following information will send shock waves up and down your spine. These statistics were compiled from Josh McDowell's website.[2]

- 50% of teens believe Jesus may have committed sins.
- 31% of born again adults agree that 'while He lived on earth, Jesus committed sins, like other people.'
- Only 9% of the 'born again' population have a Biblical worldview.
- Only 60% of U.S. born again Christians claim they've ever shared their faith with someone they knew was not a Christian.

- Almost 60% of U.S. college students today question their religious beliefs.
- A majority (52%) of all born again Christians reject the existence of the Holy Spirit.
- 39% of Americans say that Jesus Christ was crucified, but He never had a physical resurrection. Nearly the same proportion of born again Christians (35%) embrace this thinking.
- 50% of born again Christians deny Satan's existence.
- 37% of those polled are self-described Christians but are neither evangelical nor born again.
- 68% of evangelical Christians believe 'good' people of other faiths can also go to heaven.
- 26% of born again Christians believe that it doesn't matter what faith you follow because they all teach the same lessons; a belief held by 56% of non-Christians.
- Only 31% of born again Christians said they believe in moral absolutes.
- Just one out of every five born again Christians (21%) are actively involved in a discipleship process.

These findings are incredibly alarming. Not surprising, but alarming. If our pulpits are filled with godly men who believe in the inerrancy, infallibility and inspiration of Scripture, then wouldn't it make sense that they are systematically teaching the unadulterated Word of God without compromise week after week? Certainly this would be our hope. But we know this is not always the case.

There are plenty of pastors and teachers around the country who give mental and verbal ascent to the priority of Scripture, but who consistently malign it each week to fit their preferences and religious bent. And if the hearers are not Biblically in tune with what the whole counsel of God affirms, they will likely embrace whatever twisted doctrine is being peddled.

For the sake of the argument though let's just say all of the pastor's who belong to evangelical churches are preaching what I call DC (doctrinally correct). Let's assume what is being proclaimed from our pulpits is theological sound. Assuming this is the case, how would we explain the growing number of Biblically illiterate, Biblically ignorant, consumeristic, materialistic, professing Christians whose core convictions are so far removed from the basic tenants of evangelical and Biblical Christianity? Where and how is this giant disconnect taking place?

We preach. They hear, yet leave embracing heresy. What are we missing? We must ask ourselves that difficult and uncomfortable question. My fear is that we don't ask the question because we fear we will not like the answer. But it is precisely in asking the right questions that we'll get the right answers and be able to make the necessary adjustments to our plotted course, in order to appropriately invest our lives and resources in making radical disciples of all the nations.

I remember reading a book many years ago by John Fischer called *Real Christians Don't Ask Questions* (with an X through the word Don't). In it, Fischer encourages the reader to ask the hard questions because it's only in asking the hard questions that we'll get solid, satisfying answers. And if we are serious about being the passionate Christ followers that God has called us to be and if we're committed to making radical disciples of the nations, then we need to get used to asking the hard questions and responding in obedience to the answers those questions produce.

Most of us who have some church background would agree that the hard questions are by and large discouraged from being asked. So in a sense we've been conditioned in the church to show up, nod our heads, say the predictable "amen's" in all the right places, shake hands with people in our pew, and then go home and come back for more of the same thing the following week.

We seldom take the necessary time to engage people's hearts with the gut wrenching and often difficult truths found in Scripture. Similarly, we often avoid helping them process the depths of their own sin, the wonder of God's vast glory and the ramifications of God's clear call on their lives. I would suggest we often fail to help them formulate an action plan of obedience as well. Needless to say, if people can't clearly connect dots from God's Word to their own personal obedience, we cannot possibly help them grow by holding them accountable to that obedience.

A young single lady with two small children and a history of drug and alcohol abuse came in for counseling one day. I was not available to meet with her so another one of the associate pastors I worked with at the time offered to meet with this young lady. Both of us were privy to her history with men, her history with drugs, her spiritual condition, etc. My colleague met with her one time for less than an hour. I later discovered he scheduled no follow up appointments. Given her history and level of dysfunction I was a bit perplexed that he would not have planned to meet with her again. When I asked him why, he responded by saying, "She's going to be fine. She just needs to get more involved at church and start praying more."

Seriously? Is it really that simple? People with high levels of emotional and behavioral dysfunction and spiritual immaturity just need to amp up the level of church commitment and spend more time praying. Really?

Needless to say, in my mind his counsel to this young lady was tantamount to treason. Treason on our country would be no more criminal than telling a terminally ill patient that they are healthy. Why do we do this with people's spiritual lives? Often times it's because we know that dealing with people can get messy. When we start probing and asking questions of the heart it requires time and commitment. We cannot simply come alongside people, hand them a Bible verse, and move on to someone else.

I recently saw some folks throwing out plastic coins at an amusement park with John 3.16 printed on them. Are we really that naïve to believe that we can simply hand out plastic coins with Bible verses written on them and expect that to suffice? As if the assignment handed down from heaven above is simply to toss a few cursory Bible verses at people and call it all good.

Biblical, radical, God-honoring discipleship demands commitment. It requires a level of investment many are simply not willing to make. And because so many are not willing to make such a huge investment, we repackage Scripture, make it less demanding, more palatable, easier to swallow, and call it the "gospel".

On the other side of the spectrum there are many churches that have in fact considered the high cost of Biblical discipleship and have fully embraced the radical call of Jesus to come and die. I'm encouraged to hear of churches whose hearts beat for authentic Christian community and who offer Life Groups, Cell Groups, Home Groups, etc. These small groups are typically places where people can ask the genuine, hard questions about life while they learn what it means to be a radical follower of Jesus Christ. For those churches committed to authenticity, radical obedience, selfless living and sacrificial giving, and who have a heart for the nations to worship the King, I applaud you. You are setting a great model for us to follow. I'm guessing you don't have the biggest sanctuary in town. My hunch is your church budget isn't laced with fancy advertising strategies. Instead, you've relegated the bells and whistles of the mega church model and replaced that model with one that looks more like the one we find in Acts 2. For all of those reasons and so many more, I honor you.

I have a great friend who is a local pastor here in Asheville. We've been involved in his church for the past year.

My friend, Steve, is so committed to Biblical discipleship that every pastor, every elder, and everyone in leadership at his church are actively involved in one-on-one discipleship.

Studies tell us that Steve and his team are a very rare breed though. Statistics across the board reveal that most adults who claim to be followers of Christ live much like those who are not following Christ. Virtually no consistent and evident differences exist. Not surprising then that studies reveal that the vast majority of churched students walk away from their "faith" by the time they turn 25. And of those 14-19 year olds who belong to an evangelical church and participate in the church's weekly activities, an alarming number of them have very weak and faulty theology. So when that critical time comes for them to contemplate what their faith consists of and decide whether or not they will devote the totality of the rest of their lives to the cause of Christ, their decision to abandon their "faith" isn't very difficult. They really aren't walking away from much.

The bottom line is simply this – we live what we believe. Consequently, if we are not believing the right things, our behavior (how we live our lives) will no doubt be reflected by that. If our view of God is skewed, inevitably our view of ourselves, Christ, Scripture, discipleship, worship, salvation, stewardship, etc. will also be terribly distorted and our lifestyles will accurately reflect that distortion. How can we live lives of worship in the direction of a worthy Savior and Lord, when our most basic concept of His worthship is jaded? It's simply not possible.

Look around. Seriously. Look around. Listen carefully. Observe intently. What conclusions can you draw? Is there ample evidence to support the assumption that what we're doing in American Christianity is working? Are you seeing our churches take in our young children, work them through the "Youth Group" system, and then effectively send them off to be world changers? Is that happening in the churches around you? And if it is happening, is that the rule or the exception to the rule?

Are you yourself surrounded by other adults who have an insatiable passion to know Jesus and make Him known? Are you seeing adults walk away from the American Dream in exchange for a life of radical discipleship? Is your church producing disciples who are committed to being disciple makers themselves? Are the pastors, elders, and leadership teams at our churches committed to the Great Commission? And is that evidenced by their schedules, bank accounts, and the mission statements of the churches they are leading?

I'm not advocating we all assume the role of judge and jury. Certainly not. What I *am* advocating though, is that all of us who name the name of Jesus, who publicly align ourselves with Christ, who proclaim Jesus to be the Lord of our lives, should take a good, hard, honest look around us and ask ourselves if our churches are being faithful to the most basic and fundamental command of Jesus Christ to go into all the world and make disciples, teaching them how to obey. Are our churches doing that? More importantly, am I doing that and are you doing that?

Far too many churches (and professed followers of Jesus) across North America have traded in Biblical Christianity for a less abrasive, more tolerant, less costly version of the same. We seem to think we can just trade up or trade out aspects of the gospel that we find too costly or too difficult to embrace.

Jesus gave us clear warning though that many would try to circumvent the hard truths of Scripture, all the while claiming to belong to Him. And He said that one day they would stand before Him, plead their case that they rightfully belong to Him, and then list the reasons why they belong to Him. The conclusion He makes? They never belonged to Him. They were deceived into thinking they did but the harsh reality is they had no part with Him.

It's important to keep in mind, lest you think He's not referring to many of us, that Jesus is not talking about the whack-job cult leaders who claim they've had visions of Jesus leading spaceships full of aliens to our planet to rescue us from impending doom. And He's not referring to Muslims or Buddhists either. Jesus is referring to devoutly religious people who seemed to have jumped through all the right hoops, looked the part on the outside, and no doubt felt secure in their placement in the kingdom of God. Sincere folks who genuinely thought they were a part of His flock. We know people like this. They surround many of us on any given Sunday morning at church. And the painful reality is - Jesus is no doubt referring to some of us.

According to Jesus Christ, many will stand before Him and the very last words they will hear from His lips will be "I never knew you. Away from Me, you evildoers!"[3] And then they will be ushered into a dark, painful, Christless existence where they will suffer for all of eternity. This should certainly be a wake-up call for all of us because many of the people that Jesus was referring to attend our churches. It could even be that He was talking about one of us.

When we think about whether or not our churches are being faithful to Scripture, we must use the litmus test of Matthew 28 and Romans 10 as part of our evaluating. If we agree that our churches do in fact care about evangelism and discipleship, it is imperative that we ask ourselves if we are producing the kind of radical followers of Jesus Christ that He desires to use to make much of His name and renown among the nations.

Are our churches producing passionate followers of Jesus Christ whose aim it is to exhaust the totality of their lives making much of God's glory in the world? Are members of our churches willing to walk away from the comforts of their lives in order to faithfully make disciples of all the people groups across our globe? Are the characteristics I just mentioned indicative of the people who sit around us in the pew each week? The answer is painfully obvious. No!

It seems that very few of us would agree that the non-discipleship Christianity that we've been peddling from our pulpits is actually heretical. Unfortunately though, the facts speak for themselves. Instead of our strategy producing radical,

God-honoring, Christ-exalting, passionate followers of Jesus Christ, we are instead producing a mass of undisciplined, undiscipled, disobedient and Biblically ignorant pew warmers.

We know plenty enough to play the part of a nominal Christian. And we've got enough christianeze lingo down to fit in comfortably with others in our churches who are playing the same pathetic games. But at the end of the day we must ask the question - are our churches producing the kind of radical disciples that Jesus has called us to make?

It's time to stop the insanity. If we are ever going to be the church (the *ekklesia*: the called out ones) that we were designed and called to be before the foundations of the world, we must first be aggressive and brutally honest in evaluating our current paradigm. It can't stop there though. We must then be vigilant in making the necessary changes to conform to the clear revelation we find in Scripture about what it means to follow Jesus. Confession and repentance should both be a huge and vital component in our strategy to get serious about being and making disciples. More on that in later chapters.

If we don't get as serious about our heinous sin as God is, we will likely continue to repeat our folly. And I'm not just talking about our obvious sins of commission such as: gossip, envy, pride, jealousy, idolatry, laziness, bitterness, greed, and the like. I'm referring primarily to our sins of omission. When I use the term omission, I'm referring to the sins we're guilty of because we've failed to do something, whether deliberately or as a result of oversight, that the Bible has commanded us to do.

We've failed to take seriously the commands of Jesus to preach the gospel to all the world and to make disciples of all the nations. Should we choose to turn a blind eye to these sins of omission that many of us are guilty of, we will certainly repeat the vicious and dangerous cycle of propagating this false gospel that embraces and celebrates non-discipleship Christianity.

The writer of Proverbs sends out the warning like this:[4]

- "As a dog returns to its vomit, so a fool repeats his folly." NIV
- "Like a dog that returns to his vomit is a fool who repeats his folly." ESV
- "Dogs return to eat their vomit, just as fools repeat their foolishness." CEV
- "As a dog eats its own vomit, so fools recycle silliness." MSG

Some commentators would argue that this verse is talking about apostates, those who at one time partially embraced the truth claims of Scripture, but who eventually return to their former lives of blatant disobedience and darkness. It would seem logical that this verse might also be describing people who continue to repeat the same mistakes and are not vigilant to make the necessary changes so their sinful and destructive patterns of behavior stop.

When a dog throws up, whatever was in his belly that made him sick is now laying on the ground. Unknowingly, a dog will lap that infectious mucus right back up making him sick again. Kind of nasty, I agree. Proverbs says that people who exhibit this type of behavior are fools and predictably they will just continue to repeat this same destructive cycle. That is, until they rid themselves of the infection.

Let's make application here. American Christianity, with all of its bells and whistles, is essentially impotent. The classic definition of impotent would be powerless: without the strength or power to do anything effective or helpful. Of course the church isn't literally impotent in all of its various facets. But when I use the word impotent, I'm referring specifically to the churches lack of ability to penetrate the darkness and expand the kingdom. This primarily happens because we are not being faithful to the whole counsel of God by making disciples of the nations. The results we're getting from the investment we're making is woefully different from the investment and results of the church described in Acts 2 of the New Testament.

The million dollar question then is - are we willing to humble ourselves, abandon our prideful independence, declare our absolute dependence on God, and approach Scripture with a fervent desire to be radically obedient no matter what it costs us? Just for clarification, you should re-read that last sentence. Are we willing to humble ourselves, abandon our prideful independence, declare our absolute dependence on God, and approach Scripture with a fervent desire to be radically obedient no matter what it costs us?

As we hold up to the light of Scripture and test the two different paradigms we've been talking about, the real issue at hand isn't so much a matter of strategy or approach, gospel missions abroad or sports outreach programs domestically, large or small, mega-church or mini-church, preaching or teaching. It would seem the heart of the issue we're talking about is actually quality versus quantity.

Much of the crisis in the American church today can be traced back to our relentless pursuit of quantity. We're always looking for bigger, better, and more. And some even claim they want bigger, better, and more because God wants bigger, better, and more. We spend countless man hours and hundreds of millions of dollars trying to grow larger programs and increase attendance. That's simply a matter of quantity.

Instead, we should be pursuing matters of quality. Jesus invested in a few people, not because He was unable to attract the masses, but because God's master plan of recruiting worshippers rests not on accumulating the masses, but on calling and equipping the few.

The gospels are laced with vivid and detailed accounts of Jesus intentionally talking people out of the gospel. If He were primarily interested in attracting the masses, certainly He would have chosen a different and much more inclusive strategy and tolerant approach. If Jesus' primary concern was quantity as opposed to quality, His stringent and specific demands for His followers to forsake all would certainly have been more palatable and much less invasive and demanding.

If you're still reading, my guess is you're a lot like me. You desperately want to walk away from the sham of what much of American Christianity has become and you long to embrace the pure gospel, fully aware that it demands your very life. So together, let's purpose to pursue the heart of God and love Jesus with the totality of our very lives. God will be honored, His kingdom will grow, and our lives will prove that our treasure lies not in the pleasures of this world, but in the beauty and glory of a worthy King.

## OUR PRAYER

*Lord Jesus, You indeed have the words of eternal life. You have sovereignly chosen us before the world began. Before time existed You purposed to call us into existence and redeem us for Yourself.*

*For far too long we've neglected to take seriously our role as ambassadors of Jesus Christ. Instead of investing the entirety of our lives in making much of Your name among the nations, we continue to waste our lives toying with the trivialities of building our own kingdoms.*

*You've graciously given us ample warning in Your Word. You demand we renounce the heresy we've embraced for so long and embrace the pure and faultless Word of God. We've minimized the cost Jesus placed on following Him and have replaced it with a much more comfortable version of our faith.*

*We know that our actions have indeed seemed insane at times. And in fact they have been. We continue to repeat our behavior* and persist in preaching an altered gospel, all the while expecting You to use it to change the world. We confess to You our arrogant pride and stubbornness.

You are infinitely worthy of all that we have and all that we are. Teach us proper obedience to You and to Your Word. Help us to treasure You above the allures of the world. Make our hearts beat for the very things that Your heart beats for.

Today is a new day. You've given us another chance to invest our lives in Your kingdom. Empower us so we don't squander another day, another hour, yes even another minute.

Your strength is made perfect in our weakness. Our weakness demonstrates Your grace. Your grace is sufficient for today. O Lord Jesus, it is indeed an honor to know You and make You known. Give us this one consuming passion – that Your name be great among the nations.

For Jesus' sake we pray. Amen.

# 3

# WILL THE REAL JESUS PLEASE STAND

## A RADICAL CALL TO COME AND DIE

When taking a hard, honest look at the Christian landscape, as we've already discussed, we'd be hard pressed to conclude anything other than the fact that we've missed something along the way. My contention is the real problem here isn't what we're producing. Certainly a cursory glance would cause us to conclude that something is indeed wrong with the end result. And as true as this may be, we would be amiss if we only addressed the obvious problems that are just symptomatic of much deeper issues. What we're producing is purely the bi-product of the real problem. If we simply try harder to make more disciples, without recognizing and repenting of the issues at hand, we'd be just as foolish as an armless man slapping a band-aid on his severed limb and calling it all-good.

The problem at the core of this issue of non-discipleship Christianity isn't just what we're getting at the end of the assembly line; it's what we're putting in on the front end. It's unfortunate but true.

Non-discipleship Christianity permeates much of the thinking of the Westernized church. It would be safe to say that this is due to, at least in part, our rejection of absolute truth. And as soon as we reject Scripture as being the authoritative Word of God, discipleship (as Jesus defined it) is no longer mandated, but optional. Bill Hull notes, "As a result (of our adulterated view of Scripture), we have embraced a two-level Christian experience in which only serious Christians pursue and practice discipleship, while grace and forgiveness is enough for everyone else."[1] We need to keep in the forefront of our minds that Christianity without radical, Biblical discipleship is indeed Christianity without Christ.

We preach our sermons each week, whether in "big church" or in youth group and take a certain amount of pride in the fact that we wrap it up by giving a warm, inviting, benign alter call, leading would-be Christians in what we've termed the "sinner's prayer." This might be a good place to note that nowhere in all of Scripture is the sinner's prayer found. Nowhere. For all of us who are guilty of it, our souls should be grieved that we've reduced the gospel and the radical call of Jesus to come and die, to a simple 30 second prayer to "invite Jesus into our hearts." The radical gospel simply demands more than this.

We all need to be clear about this. As warm and inviting as the sinner's prayer might be, it more often than not misses the heart of Jesus' call for His potential followers to come and die. It simply offers a cheapened gospel by making available the benefits of salvation without explaining the cost of our

72

allegiance to Christ. And when we propagate this heresy, we further perpetuate a corrupt and faulty version of the gospel. We say, in essence, all that it takes to get "in" is simply praying a prayer inviting Jesus into your heart. And then once we get them "in," we coddle them and make them feel like it's all about them. Years later, we discover the vast majority of these folks have either walked away or continue to warm our pews, having no impact on the kingdom.

You and I both know far too many people who prayed the prayer, walked the isle, and have since either checked out or who sit comfortably, unmoved and unchanged, in the same seat every Sunday morning of the year. They may sing the songs and perhaps even offer up a few "amen's" occasionally. But there is no transformation happening. There is no fruit being produced in their lives. And there is nothing to indicate their hearts have ever been captivated by the Savior of the world.

Please hear me clearly. I am in no way saying that I don't want people to be genuinely converted to Christianity. I do! I long to see people's lives transformed by the salvific gospel of Jesus Christ. I've devoted the entirety of my life to this end. However, we've turned the radical, life altering, costly call of Jesus to follow Him into a drive-thru request for a better tomorrow.

Certainly there are many benefits to living in a proper relationship with God by having an authentic relationship with Jesus. No doubt about it. But, let's not forget the method, means, and message Jesus employed when He called people to repent. Time after time throughout the gospels we see Jesus calling people to consider the high cost of following Him. Many, if not most, clearly walked away from Jesus simply because He required too much. The cost was too high. The price tag was more than they were willing to spend.

Jesus no doubt created space in the temple, along the shore, and on the mountainsides of Judea and Galilee when He beckoned people to take up their crosses and follow Him. And we will likewise create space in the pews in our churches when we deliver the pure, unadulterated gospel of Jesus Christ, making clear the high cost of following Jesus. We're not peddling a coupon book with a fast pass to heaven. We're beckoning people to lay down their lives, die to themselves, and embrace a radical, selfless life of total surrender to the cause of Christ.

Caveat - where are the prophets in this generation? Where are these fearless men who will boldly stand and proclaim a faultless gospel detailing man's wicked sin, a worthy Redeemer, and His call on all of humanity to come and die? Where are the men who will cast the net, not as a manipulated means of selling fire insurance, but an unapologetic call to walk away from the allures of this world and recklessly follow this crazy man Jesus? Where are these men?

In light of the adulterated gospel that we've peddled for so long, is it even surprising then that most of our churches have adopted the two-level system of Christianity I mentioned earlier? It shouldn't surprise us in the least. It should rather alarm us at the core. Once we've been made painfully aware of our deviance from the heart of Scripture, we should be sickened by all the years we've wasted pimping out this polluted and Christless gospel. It is really no gospel at all.

Here's the gospel: Jesus stands before a dying world with a penetrating indictment – we stand guilty before a holy God. All of us, not just the "bad" people. He stands before the entire world (that includes the likes of Mother Theresa and Adolf Hitler and everyone in between) claiming to be God incarnate and He says some crazy things like, "I and the Father are one." "If you know Me, you know My Father." "For My Father's will is that everyone who looks to the Son and believes in Him shall have eternal life." "I am the way, the truth and the life and no one gets to My Father except through Me. And when I say no one, I mean no one."[2]

Some of these statements are fairly easy to swallow. We don't have too much trouble acknowledging that God and Jesus are one. We're okay jumping on board with those evangelicals by saying Jesus is the way to God. We can live with that. Some would argue whether He's the *only* way to God though. There are some nice, church going people who are very reluctant to say that sincere people of other faiths are going to hell. Some of us have an equally difficult time acknowledging that people within our own ranks are going to a Christless eternity. The statistics I mentioned earlier reveal that an alarming 68% of evangelical Christians believe that good people of other faiths can also go to heaven.

When it comes to salvation, we simply have trouble embracing an intolerant and exclusive Jesus. And so instead of allowing Scripture to dictate to us who Jesus really is, we cast our image of a safe and benign Jesus onto the pages of Scripture. Instead of seeing Jesus through the lens of the Word of God, we allow our idealized version of Jesus to be the lens through which we attempt to interpret the Word. It goes without saying this method of interpretation is incredibly foolish, dangerous, and undermines the glorious gospel of Jesus Christ and the wisdom of God. Not to mention it creates a version of Jesus that is inconsistent with the Jesus of the Bible.

What about the rest of what Jesus said? Why is it that we're willing to take the little, coated, get-out-of-hell-free, easy to swallow pills, but we're not so willing to put down the horse tablets? When talking about the gospel, we do not have the liberty of picking and choosing what we want to believe and what we would like to discard. That's just not a luxury we've been afforded. Do many people do it? Absolutely. But those of us who are committed to the authority of Scripture and following hard after Jesus must be diligent to ensure our lives conform to the desires of Jesus Himself.

Here are some of the not-so-easy-to-swallow statements that rolled off of the lips of Jesus when He beckoned people to follow Him. Things like:

- *"If anyone comes to Me and doesn't hate his family, and even his own life, he cannot be My disciple."* **Luke 14.26**
- *"Whoever does not bear his own cross and come after Me cannot be My disciple."* **Luke 14.27**
- *"Any of you that does not renounce all that He has cannot be My disciple."* **Luke 14.33**

76

- *"Go into all the world and proclaim the gospel to the whole creation."* **Mark 16.15**
- *"Whoever would be great among you must be your servant."* **Mark 10.43**
- *"If anyone would come after Me, let him deny himself and take up his cross and follow Me. For whoever would save his life will lose it, but whoever loses his life for My sake and the gospel's will save it."* **Mark 8.34-35; Matthew 16.24-26**
- *"I have all authority. Go and make disciples of all nations...teaching them to obey what I've commanded you."* **Matthew 28.16-20**
- *"Whoever loves father or mother more than Me is not worthy of Me, and whoever loves son or daughter more than Me is not worthy of Me. And whoever does not take his cross and follow Me is not worthy of Me. Whoever finds his life will lose it, and whoever loses his life for My sake will find it."* **Matthew 10.37-39**
- *"No one can serve two masters. Either he will hate the one and love the other, or he will be devoted to the one and despise the other."* **Matthew 6.24**
- *"Repent..."* **Matthew 4.17**

It is these verses and so many others like them that cause me great anguish over the apparent discrepancies in my own life and ministry. If I believe these words of Jesus then I must constantly and vigilantly wage war with the American, consumeristic version of Christianity that plagues our culture and has invaded our churches. I must be dogmatic when it comes to rejecting anything that reeks of the stench of our adulterated Americanized Christianity while running towards and embracing the hard claims of Jesus. No easy task in America. Or anywhere for that matter.

I'm also anguished because I don't see many pastors and youth pastors who seem to be waging this same war. I'm not sure if those I've locked arms with in ministry over the years are genuine allies or enemies of the cross, masquerading as those in the light. Isn't it true that we're either for God or against Him? That means we either embrace and believe the hard sayings of Jesus or we don't. There is no neutral territory here. And my heart is anguished because as I look around and listen to those behind the microphones, I hear more pep rally jargon and come-and-get-it crap than the clarion call of Jesus to come and die.

Seems we've been inadvertently sucked into this American, Westernized version of Christianity, where the goal is to feel good, get more stuff, be more comfortable, have nicer things, and enjoy all of God's richest 'blessings' in this life. I can possibly see how finding a select few verses would lead us to this temporal and overtly shallow goal. But I cannot fathom how someone looking at the whole counsel of God can come to these same deluded conclusions.

Dietrich Bonhoeffer said, "One cannot be a disciple of Christ without forfeiting things normally sought in human life, and that one who pays little in the world's coinage to bear His name has reason to wonder where he or she stands with God."[3]

Listen, aligning yourself with Jesus and taking seriously His call on your life will be costly. No doubt about it. And let's be clear - a commitment to be and make disciples must be the intentional central act of every follower of Jesus Christ and every church scattered across the globe. Period.

The more I pursue Christ, the more He illuminates the diseases of my heart, the vast dysfunction of my soul, and the glory of the beautiful gospel. As much as I would love the quick fixes for my thorns in the flesh, my defects, my dysfunctions, and my miserable failings, the truth is Christ has given me none. He has allowed me to see a glimpse of His majesty and my desperate need for Him, while equipping me with the grace and mercy I need for today.

Before we can understand the true nature of Biblical discipleship we must first have a clear understanding of who this Jesus is that is doing the calling. If the lens through which we see Him is blurred and if our view of Him is altered, our understanding and interpretation of His radical call will likewise be misaligned. And such is the case today.

Of course, every book in the Bible ultimately exists to make much of Jesus. Some do that more clearly and more directly than others. The Apostle John penned these words, "Now there are also many other things that Jesus did. Were every one of them to be written, I suppose that the world itself could not contain the books that would be written."[4] There is more pertaining to His eternal existence and incarnation than we could ever capture in centuries of recorded media. However, for a synopsis of the life and intentions of Jesus Christ, we'd certainly look first at the four gospels. They detail His life, His ministry, His passions, His burdens, His death, His burial, His resurrection, His ascension, His second coming and everything in between.

The book you're holding is written with a particular view of His radical call on all of humanity to follow hard after Him. As we've mentioned before, somewhere down through the years we've misconstrued His mandates on our lives as optional suggestions for a better tomorrow. The truth is though, embracing Jesus Christ and purposing to follow hard after Him will most definitely wreck every facet of your life.

Two thousand years ago, few actually embraced the radical call of Jesus and were able to see the significant implications this call would have on their lives. Some did. And God wisely used the few who did to turn the world upside down. We are here, in large part, because of a few unlikely men (and women) who were willing to walk away from the life they knew in exchange for the life He promised. And lest we're tempted to succumb to some aspect of the perverted prosperity gospel, we should keep in mind the life Jesus offered was promised to be saturated with trouble and heartache. Yes, there are some great promises of joy in the morning and eternity in the presence of Christ. But between here and there, the road is often marked with suffering. No doubt the road occasionally seems long and sometimes very wearisome. That's one of the reasons the writer of Hebrews tells us that this High Priest we follow, this Christ who has won our allegiance, is not immune to the hardships and sufferings in life. He Himself is able to sympathize with our weaknesses because He too has quite literally walked in our shoes.[5]

It would be futile and I'd be amiss to attempt to sum up the life of Jesus and simplify it to a single sentence or theme. And I'm definitely not attempting to do that here. For the sake of clarity though, I'd like to remind you that the Bible is a book about discipleship, written by disciples to disciples for disciples.

Although the gospels provide a myriad of passages and verses detailing the call of Jesus to consider the exorbitant cost of following Him, we should point out that nowhere in Scripture is the mandate and cost more poignant than in Matthew 28. We'll take a closer look at this passage later, but for now we should note that in Matthew 28.18, Jesus makes it abundantly clear that He is the One who holds the power to call the shots. It is Jesus Himself that possesses every single ounce of authority and power. And, before He hands down the mandate, He states the obvious – He alone has the authority to make the decisions and demand a response. He alone carries the title of Ruler, Master, and Lord. And as Ruler of the universe and Lord of our lives, we owe our allegiance to Him. Not just to those things that are comfortable and easy to either embrace or abandon, but we owe our total allegiance to Him, even when the cost is great and the stakes are high.

I cannot think of anything in all of life where the cost could be greater or the stakes higher than purposing to invest the totality of our lives in being a disciple and making other disciples. There are very few things in all of Scripture that are so weighty. Everything we do, everything we will ever be, hinges on our understanding of and acceptance of this mandate from Jesus to follow hard after Him.

## OUR PRAYER

*Father God, You have indeed given us the Light of the world so we are no longer walking in darkness. You have redeemed our lives and removed the scales from our eyes so we can see clearly the glory of the gospel.*

*We often celebrate the benefits of the gospel with little or no consideration of the demands placed on those of us who profess our allegiance with Christ. We've misconstrued and magnified the advantages of knowing Christ and have virtually eliminated any mention of the requirements and responsibilities of following Him.*

*In our efforts to see souls redeemed, we've neutered the clear words of the gospel of Jesus Christ. While trying to appease those whose hearts are set against Christ, we've embraced a highly polluted and pain-free form of Christianity and veraciously proclaimed it as truth from our pulpits and classrooms.*

*O God, we stand guilty before You of cheapening the depth and despair of our sin, and subsequently minimizing the richness of Your grace and Your mercy. All the while, we've also ignored many of the demands Jesus places on His followers.*

*Our sin has influenced others. We've propagated a perverted and adulterated gospel, which is really no gospel at all. And in the process we've brought reproach to Your name. We confess this as the heinous sin for which it is.*

*Righteous Lord, help us to embrace the hard truths we find in Your Word. Don't allow us to run from the high cost of following Jesus. Instead, deepen our love for You and Your Word so that we gladly embrace all that Jesus taught. We know that it's only in losing our lives that we'll truly find them. And it's only in taking up our cross and following You that we'll be counted worthy of bearing Your name.*

*Jesus, we agree that You are indeed the way, the truth and the life, and that apart from You people cannot know God. You alone stand before the world as the only worthy Mediator between God and mankind. Mark us with a genuine burden and a great desire to carry the gospel to all those who have still never heard. And graciously empower us to make disciples who are as zealous for Your honor as You are.*

*Anoint our steps and our speech, for the glory of Your name. Amen.*

# A DIVISIVE LINE IN THE SAND

## IT'S CLEAR WE'RE NOT ALL ON THE SAME SIDE

We live in a culture that celebrates peace and diversity. If you want to make enemies, do anything or say anything that would cause others to think you're a narrow minded, arrogant, intolerant human being. Claiming to have some exclusive angle on truth will quickly take you off the list of Barbara Walters' 10 Most Fascinating People. Say something that suggests that all paths do not lead to God, and you'll be branded as one of those intolerant Christian extremists. A modern day John the Baptist.

There certainly are real extremists out there doing some pretty insane things, all in the name of "God." Total whack jobs to the core. Guys like Jim Jones, David Koresh, and Marshall Applewhite, to name a few. Let me share with you a little about each of these guys to be sure there is no confusion when we talk about living radical lives for the glory of God.

On April 19, 1993 David Koresh (born Vernon Howell) claimed the lives of 80 of his Branch Davidian followers, including 25 children, in what seemed to be their final trial by fire. The 33 year old self-proclaimed "Lamb of God" thus ended a 51 day standoff with federal law enforcement.

That standoff began February 28th when agents of the Bureau of Alcohol, Tobacco, and Firearms (ATF) attempted to serve Koresh with a warrant at his Davidian compound outside Waco, Texas. This effort erupted in gunfire. Heavily armed Davidians fired upon federal agents killing four and wounding 16 ATF agents. After the shootout, Koresh refused to leave the enclosure often called "Ranch Apocalypse." The FBI assumed control of the perimeter and conducted negotiations. David Koresh repeatedly broke his promises to come out peacefully. A frustrated and exhausted FBI subsequently attempted to end the standoff by gassing the compound. Koresh, then forced to choose between his compound Kingdom and certain criminal prosecution, opted to end not only his own life, but that of his followers as well.

This was the tragic end of Koresh's six year rule over the once benign Davidian sect. David Koresh was a man many mental health experts were inclined to describe as a likely "psychopath."

On November 18, 1978 over 900 followers of American cult leader Jim Jones ("Peoples Temple") died in a remote South American jungle compound called "Jonestown" in British Guyana. Some members were shot, others were forced to drink poison, but most willingly participated in what Jones said was an act of "revolutionary suicide."

Anticipating the end of his ministry and certain arrest, Jim Jones ordered the "state of emergency" he had so long anticipated. This carefully rehearsed mass suicide now finally took place. Everyone, except the very few that escaped into the surrounding jungle, either committed suicide or was murdered. Sadly, more than 280 children were killed. Jim Jones' body was found at Jonestown, fatally wounded by a gunshot to the head.

In March of 1997 thirty nine people, 21 women and 18 men were found dead in a mansion within the exclusive neighborhood of Rancho Santa Fe near San Diego in the United States. They ranged in age from 26 to 72 and came from nine different states within the US. The thirty nine bodies were identified as members of a cult group, which later came to be known as "Heaven's Gate."

The bodies were found dispersed within the mansion on cots and mattresses. All but two had shrouds of purple covering their heads and shoulders. Most died of suffocation, induced by plastic bags placed over their heads, after taking a concoction of Phenobarbital and alcohol. Found among the dead was Marshall Herff Applewhite, the 65 year old leader of the group.[1]

These are just three examples of some of the modern day extremist's, who commit terrible crimes and unconscionable acts, all in the name of "God." And just to be clear, when I advocate living outrageously radical lives, taking crazy risks, and wasting our lives on the kingdom, I'm talking about doing all of those things (and more!) as they line up with the revealed Word of God. I'm in no way advocating that you take these calculated risks while following some charismatic nut job who claims he has some special revelation from God. If you ever find yourself in a situation like this, you should run away fast.

I don't want to make light of this situation, because many unsuspecting people have become entangled and entrapped in cults and cult-like groups. If you or someone you know is in a cult or have questions about what a cult is, I've listed some helpful resources for you.[2] I've also included a check list of sorts to help you identify the normal characteristics of a cult.[3]

When I talk about being branded as a Christian extremist, I'm actually not being facetious. If you take seriously the claims of Christ and adhere to His teaching, you will most certainly be branded as intolerant, narrow-minded, extremist, dangerous, etc, etc, etc.

Jesus was branded, the prophets before Him were branded, and the disciples after Him were branded. As we purpose to follow hard after Jesus and adhere to His teachings and the teachings of the early apostles, should we expect anything less for ourselves?[4] Of course, if you listen to proponents of mainstream American Christianity, you'll hear some outrageous claims advocating a trouble free life of ease and material abundance that Christians are supposedly entitled to.

Don't feel bad though if you get branded as one of those narrow minded Jesus freaks. The truth is, Jesus was not only a member, He was the President and CEO of the "Narrow Minded, Arrogant, Exclusive, Intolerant" Club. Since He's God, He could be the self-appointed President of such a club without ever even doing anything. But such is not the case with Him. He's not just the self-appointed President of the club, who serves from afar. He currently occupies this position from the chambers of heaven, but only after spending many years on planet earth making some outrageously controversial claims.

We'd be hard pressed to find anything seemingly more narrow minded and intolerant than what Jesus articulated in John 14.6. Referring to Himself and with His own lips He uttered these words - "I am *the* way and *the* truth and *the* life. *No one* comes to the Father except through Me."

I can't think of anything in all of Scripture that would appear more intolerant than Jesus' assertion that He alone exclusively held the position as the one and only way to get to God. He didn't say there were a hundred ways. Nor did He say there were twelve ways. Jesus didn't say there were even two ways. Jesus said there was one and only one way to have access to the first person of the Trinity, God the Father, and that was by way of having a relationship with the second person of the Trinity, God the Son, namely Himself.

Exclusive? Absolutely. Intolerant? Of course. Narrow minded? Without a doubt. Does it all sound a bit arrogant? You bet. So then what do we make of all this? Welcome to the Biblical version of Christianity and the narrow gate that leads to God-honoring, Christ-exalting, radical discipleship.

This certainly has the potential to be polarizing. And in fact, it is indeed polarizing. But, I don't make the rules here and neither do you. If life were set up so that we could make up our own rules and live by them, I'd be the first one to speak out against anything that would cause division and hate. I'd be sounding the alarm calling on all of my fellow American's to celebrate tolerance. I'd join all the marches in Washington, DC to promote agendas of unity and peace. I would have long ago become an environmental activist or animal activist or social activist. Perhaps even joined Joel Osteen's staff to help promote everyone's best life now.

But the world we live in isn't set up that way. I don't get to make up my own rules to live by. And neither do you. If we did, I'm afraid we'd all be in a catastrophic heap of trouble. Think about it. Everyone making their own rules to live by and doing what seems right in their own eyes. This all might seem incredibly inviting and rather appealing at first. But imagine the following, not so far-fetched, scenario:

I think we should all wear black on Fridays. You think everyone should wear shorts on Mondays. Your dad doesn't think we should be wearing anything at all. Ever! He's a self-professed nudist. I don't think anyone in America should be able to drive cars that cost more than the average home. You think we should all ride scooters. My neighbor thinks we should all walk in an effort to help eliminate global warming. I believe all kids should go to private schools. You advocate all Christian families should home school. My long lost cousin, Vinney, thinks we should close down all the schools and let kids learn on their own, from the school of hard knocks. I'm of the mindset that stealing from the local market can't be condemned if no one gets hurt. Sherriff Rollins thinks sharing should be an enforceable law. I think every person that smokes in a car carrying passengers should be arrested for attempted murder. You believe people should be able to smoke in the mall and our government should legalize marijuana and change the legal drinking age to twelve. And all of my kids think ice cream and sour patch kids should be served with every meal.

It all seems a bit far-fetched, but you see where this would lead. It wouldn't be a good idea if we all got to make up our own rules. It might sound good in theory, but in practice I'm sure you'd quickly concede it would be a horrific nightmare with catastrophic repercussions.

I remember sitting next to Woody Harrelson one time on a flight from Denver to Rapid City, South Dakota. Woody Harrelson is an actor for whom real life is undeniably stranger than his movie roles. Woody is the son of a convicted murderer, veteran of multiple arrests, outspoken environmentalist, and tireless hemp proponent. He's best known for his role on the TV sitcom *Cheers*, although he's also starred in a variety of movies like *Casualties of War, Doc Hollywood, White Men Can't Jump, Indecent Proposal* and *Natural Born Killers*.

When I sat down beside him on the plane, he instantly pulled a small cotton bag out of his backpack and offered me some hemp. I respectfully declined. He actually put it in his mouth and chewed on it. Not exactly sure what that was about, but that's the way it shook down.

Shortly after we got settled, I began praying that God would give me an opportunity to share the gospel with Woody. Within a matter of minutes we both lined up our questions and began firing them off, one after the other. This went on for nearly an hour and a half.

Interestingly, Woody told me that he grew up in a "Christian" home and went to church regularly. The trajectory of his early life is not unlike that of millions of teenagers around the country today who grow up in similar homes with similar church attendance.

I'll never forget it. When we started talking about sin, he made it clear that he didn't think there was any such thing. He believed everyone should be able to do whatever they want without anyone telling them otherwise.

I asked Woody if he had kids. He does indeed have children. So I asked him what he would think if his daughter came home from school one day and told him that it was going to be her senior project to sleep with every guy in high school before she graduated. I asked him if he'd be okay with that. Of course, after he thought about it briefly he realized where I was going with my question and quickly conceded that it wouldn't be okay for his daughter to do that. Prior to posing this hypothetical scenario to him though, he thought it would be good for everyone to live by their own rules, much like he had grown accustomed to doing himself.

It's a good thing we don't actually have the liberty to make our own rules to govern our lives by. The fact is many of those have been made for us.

And it's pretty much the same when it comes to spiritual things, too. We don't have to, or get to for that matter, make the rules and guidelines to govern our lives by. They have been made for us. Scripture is clear in so many areas. Granted, there are some gray areas that have heartfelt proponents on both sides. But, we're not talking about the gray areas here. We're talking about black and white issues that really leave no room for debate. The bottom line is there are many who are woefully maligning the Word of God and the call of Jesus.

Jesus stands before every person on this globe, and speaking on behalf of His Father, says things like:

- *"Not everyone who says to Me 'Lord, Lord' will enter the kingdom of heaven."*[5]
- *"Behold I am sending you out as sheep in the midst of wolves, so be wise as serpents and as innocent as doves. Beware of men, for they will deliver you over to courts and flog you in their synagogues, and you will be dragged before governors and kings for My sake, to bear witness before them and the Gentiles."*[6]
  *you = radical followers of Christ
- *"You will be hated by all for My name's sake."*[7]
- *"There will be a final judgment, a day of reckoning."*[8]
- *"Some hear the Word, but the cares of this world and the deceitfulness of riches and the desire for things choke it out and make it unfruitful."*[9]

It's astonishingly clear from Scripture that we can't possibly be the extension of Jesus to this lost and dying world, delivering a message of reconciliation to the billions of people who don't know Christ, while we hold so tightly to the allures and riches of this world. We simply cannot serve two masters.[10] We will either be devoted to our riches and the wealth of this world and walk away from Christ, or we'll loosen our death grip on the fleeting pleasures this world affords and embrace the radical life we've been called to. Hanging on to our riches and following hard after Jesus seem to be at odds with each other.

And before we get all haughty and self-righteous about the amount we gave to charity last year, we should all keep something in mind. We will not be held accountable for how much we gave away, but rather on what we kept for ourselves. The stinging reality of that truth alone has the potential to change much of the kingdom influence we are able to have in terms of global evangelism, missions, and discipleship. However, that will only happen if we recognize and obediently respond to the fact that the resources we have belong to Him and He requires that we use them to build His kingdom, not ours.

I know Oprah has done so much good for so many people around the world. Most notably, she started an all girls school in South Africa that is home to some three hundred girls. While there is much good to be said for her endeavor in South Africa, spiritually speaking, we'd be misled and blinded to think that God is going to reward her philanthropic endeavors while she rests extravagantly in her custom built fifty million dollar home or in one of her many luxurious mansions scattered around the world.

Bill Gates is another incredibly wealthy person who has certainly done a lot of good for a large number of people. And by the standards of the world he should be saluted, honored, and crowned as a true hero. And perhaps he is a true hero.

Again though, looking at this through the lens of Scripture, we'd be hard pressed to find a precedent where Jesus honors the one who gave from his abundance. Quite the opposite, in fact. Jesus esteems and honors those who give, not out of their abundance, but with a generous and sacrificial heart.[11]

How do rich people give sacrificially and still live in luxury? I'm not sure. Perhaps that's one of the reasons Jesus said it's easier for a camel to go through the eye of a needle than for a rich person to enter into heaven.[12] To live with excess seems to contradict the necessary requirements of being a radical disciple of Christ who is willing to invest the whole of their lives in building the Kingdom of God.

Can I ask a favor? Please don't write me nasty letters accusing me of being unchristlike and judging Oprah and Bill Gates. I'm not judging them nor am I judging you. Scripture is clear that the title and role of judge belongs to the only One wise enough to pronounce fair and impartial judgment on the world and the inhabitants of it. Oprah and Bill can spend their money however they want. And so can we. But before we do we should be informed and understand clearly that Jesus has called every follower of His to invest their financial resources generously and sacrificially on building His kingdom. And before we spend the money we've worked so hard to accumulate, we should take another look at the Scripture that teaches us that whatever we do for others, we are actually doing for Jesus Himself. And what we fail to do for others, we've neglected to do for Him.[13]

We must also keep in mind that God, as rightful Owner of everything, is the One who gives wealth. According to 1 Samuel 2.6-8, He alone makes people rich and makes people poor. We can conclude then that everything we have comes from God and belongs to God.

The apostle Paul said that the love of money is the root of all evil.[14] He didn't say money itself was evil, but the love of money was the root of the evil. He wasn't condemning having money, he was condemning the desire to accumulate and hoard wealth.

When talking to the rich young man who wanted to know what it would take for him to get into heaven, Jesus responded to the man by telling him he would have to let loose of his possessions and walk away from his belongings in order to be fit to follow after Him.[15]

Jesus told a would-be disciple interested in following Him that He (Jesus) had no place to lay His head.[16] The most influential Leader that ever stepped on this globe and the renegade Principal of the most powerful movement in history had no bed of His own. It wasn't that His home was smaller than that of the High Priests or that His haven wasn't equal to some of the religious leaders of His time. It was that He didn't have a place to call home. Caesar had no physical address for Jesus on file.

Certainly as the most powerful Man to ever live, He could have easily paved the way for us and laid the foundation as an example of all that we are entitled to as His followers. Right?

Jesus could have affirmed our natural desire to lay up treasures here on earth. He could have personally accumulated material riches and then told us to go and do likewise. He certainly could have done all of that and more.

Instead though, He chose to model a life unattached to the things of this world. He chose to reject the alluring trappings of material possessions and He embraced a life in which the focus was on laying up treasure in heaven. He unapologetically denounced accumulating possessions for personal and selfish consumption. A life we have clearly and without question been called to emulate.

This is precisely where I think many self-professed evangelicals get off track and begin down a very dangerous road, possibly initially paved with good intentions, but underlain with the deception and evil intent that could only come from Satan himself. While many of us live oblivious to it all, Satan masquerades like an angel of light, deceiving millions by blinding their eyes to the glory of the pure gospel.

It is not my intent to single out any individual or any particular denomination in my explanation of this dividing line in the sand. While some pretend there is no dividing line and others call for more unity and greater patience while we labor together in the gospel, it must be stated and made clear that we are not all laboring in the same gospel as so many falsely assume.

I don't doubt that there will be differences in interpretations and I'm not so naïve to think we're all going to agree on every nuance in Scripture. But the different gospels we proclaim have much greater discrepancies than might initially meet the eyes and more than most of us are comfortable acknowledging. And I'm not referring to the vast chasm that exists between Christianity and Buddhism or Christianity and Islam. I'm talking about the gulf that exists between mainstream, evangelical Christians who are all presumably teaching and preaching the gospel of Jesus Christ.

We do the kingdom of God a monumental disservice when we don't package the gospel correctly and when we malign the Word of God, no matter the reason. The truth is, I don't like to think of people like Benny Hinn, TD Jakes, Joyce Meyer, and Joel Osteen as peddler's of a false gospel. It's difficult for me to look at people like Rod Parsley and Robert Schuller and know they are being used as pawns of the Enemy. But, it's impossible to conclude otherwise.

Schuller, founder of the Crystal Cathedral in Garden Grove California, when responding to the churches recent decision to file Chapter 11, said "Tough times never last, but tough people do!" Of course, this is also the title of one of Schuller's best-selling books. He has another book called "Why Bad Things Happen to Good People". I'm just wondering what Bible he reads. How can you possibly walk away from the 66 books of the Old and New Testaments and conclude that tough times don't last? How is it that one can conclude that tough people are the ones who survive? I mean, really? So as pastors then, we just need to help our people toughen up. And we need to help them see why bad things are happening to them, in spite of how good they are. Perhaps you can see why my level of concern is so high, and why red lights flash and alarms buzz every time I hear someone like Schuller behind a microphone or peddling another one of his heretical books.

Hey listen, I'd also like to think we're all basically good people and that we all deserve good things. But, doesn't the Bible teach us just the opposite? Aren't we taught in Romans 3.10 that no one is good? No one is righteous. Not even one of us! We have all turned against God. If this is true then, how can I *not* conclude that people like Robert Schuller and I are on different sides of the fence? I must conclude we are in fact, on polar opposite sides of the gospel. As you listen, read, and watch, keep in mind that regardless of current religious trends and fashions, Jesus has indeed drawn a line in the sand and invited us to join Him on His side.

Creflo Dollar, famed pastor of The World Changers Church International, said in a recent interview "God wants us to prosper in every arena and He wants us to be successful so that we can prove to people that there is profit in serving God. He wants you to have a prosperous life. Why? Because He loves you." Do I even need to explain how jacked up this is?

Mr. Dollar has convinced himself and is convincing millions of others that God is blessing us so that people will see there is material reward and gain for loving and serving God. On the homepage of his website it states as part of his mission statement, "from finances to walking in divine health; Creflo Dollar Ministries is committed to equipping people all over the world with the knowledge and wisdom needed to make decisions that will positively impact their futures."

If Mr. Dollar is going to live in a multi-million dollar home and drive a Bentley, he is no doubt compelled to figure out a way to justify his lavish lifestyle by twisting Scripture to make sense of it all. How else could he justify maintaining such an extravagant standard of living while so many around the world are literally starving to death?

Keep in mind that all of the men (except John) who walked most closely with Jesus during His time on earth were all brutally executed. They lost their heads, were skinned alive, boiled in oil, and drug through town. John died alone while exiled on an island. Is it logical to conclude that these men made decisions that 'positively impacted their futures'?

According to Mr. Dollar and many others like him, Christianity was only costly for the early disciples and those currently living in communist, anti-Christian countries. How does this health, wealth, and prosperity message work in remote villages of Ethiopia and the cold cellars of communist China? It simply doesn't work there. No matter how much faith these die-hard Christians in China and Africa can muster up, they will never have the bigger and better as promised by the bogus health, wealth, and prosperity trash.

We all need to wise up and recognize rubbish for what it is. If this twisted, perverted, adulterated gospel actually works and if it actually represents the heart of God, wouldn't it be critical that Mr. Dollar and all the other proponents of this health, wealth, and prosperity junk spend much more time and exhaust their ministry resources in places like Africa where upwards of 30,000 children starve to death every single day? If this garbage they peddle truly is the heart of God, isn't it critically imperative that they take this message to the remote villages up the tributaries of Peru and Ecuador and to all the remote villages across the continent of Africa?

They can't take this message to these people, because even if these unsuspecting people heard this message and believed it, they would still be poor and their children would still be starving to death. And the health, wealth, and prosperity gospel would be exposed for what it truly is, nothing short of a sham that seeks to exploit and deceive for purely selfish gain.

I know I sound a bit cynical about all of this. I'm really not trying to be. I'm actually grieved. My heart hurts when I hear these guys talk, because I know they are deceiving so many lives on their lucrative and plush pathway to prosperity.

I appreciate other ministers who are courageous enough to stand up and expose the health, wealth, and prosperity gospel for what it really is. John MacArthur and John Piper are two of these men. The following excerpt is from an article John MacArthur wrote called *A Colossal Fraud* that can be found on MacArthur's website.[17]

"Someone needs to say this plainly: The faith healers and health-and-wealth preachers who dominate religious television are shameless frauds. Their message is not the true gospel of Jesus Christ. There is nothing spiritual or miraculous about their on-stage chicanery. It is all a devious ruse designed to take advantage of desperate people. They are not godly ministers but greedy impostors who corrupt the Word of God for money's sake. They are not real pastors who shepherd the flock of God but hirelings whose only design is to fleece the sheep. Their love of money is glaringly obvious in what they say as well as how they live. They claim to possess great spiritual power, but in reality they are rank materialists and enemies of everything holy.

There is no reason anyone should be deceived by this age-old con, and there is certainly no justification for treating the hucksters as if they were authentic ministers of the gospel. Religious charlatans who make merchandise of false promises have been around since the apostolic era. They pretend to be messengers of Christ, but they are interlopers and impostors. The apostles condemned them with the harshest possible language. Paul called them "men of corrupt minds and destitute of the truth, who suppose that godliness is a means of gain" (1 Timothy 6.5). Peter called them false prophets with "hearts trained in greed" (2 Peter 2.14). He warned that "in their greed they will exploit you with false words" (v3). He exposed them as scoundrels and dismissed them as "stains and blemishes" on the church (v13).

Those biblical descriptions certainly fit the greed-driven cult of prosperity preachers and faith healers who unfortunately, thanks to television, have become the best-known face of Christianity worldwide. The scam they operate ought to be a bigger scandal than any Wall Street ponzi scheme or big-time securities fraud. After all, those who are most susceptible to the faith-healers' swindle are not well-to-do investors but some of society's most vulnerable people—including multitudes who are already destitute, disconsolate, disabled, elderly, sick, suffering, or dying. The faith-healer gets lavishly rich while the victims become poorer and more desperate.

But the *worst* part of the scandal is that it's not really a scandal at all in the eyes of most evangelical Christians. Those who should be most earnest in defense of the truth have taken a shockingly tolerant attitude toward the prosperity preachers' blatant misrepresentation of the gospel and their wanton exploitation of needy people. "*But we don't want to judge*," they say. Thus Christians fail to exercise *righteous* judgment (John 7.24). They refuse to be discerning at all."

There's also a short video on YouTube of John Piper talking about this prosperity gospel. It's a five minute clip every church in the world should show on the most attended Sunday morning of the year. In it, Piper says:

"I don't know what you feel about the prosperity gospel - the health, wealth, and prosperity gospel. But I'll tell you what I feel about it. Hatred. It is not the gospel. And it's being exported from this country to Africa and Asia. Selling a bill of goods to the poorest of the poor. Believe this message and your pigs won't die and your wife won't have miscarriages, and you'll have rings on your fingers and coats on your back. That's coming out of America. The people that ought to be giving our money and our time and our lives. Instead, selling a bunch of crap called gospel. And here's the reason it is so horrible: When was the last time that any American, African, Asian ever said "Jesus is all satisfying" because you drove a BMW? Never! They'll say "Did Jesus give you that? Well I'll take Jesus." That's idolatry, that's not the gospel. That's elevating gifts above Giver. I'll tell you what makes Jesus look beautiful. It's when you smash your car and your little girl goes flying through the windshield and lands dead on the street, and you say, through the deepest possible pain, 'God is enough. He is good. He will take care of us. He will satisfy us. He will get us through this. He is our Treasure. Whom have I in heaven but You? And on earth there is nothing that I desire besides You. My heart and my flesh and my little girl may fail, but You are the strength of my heart and my portion forever.' That makes God look glorious. As God, not as giver of cars or safety or health. Oh how I pray that America would be purged of the health, wealth, and prosperity gospel and that the Christian church would be marked by suffering for Christ. God is most glorified in you when you are most satisfied in Him, in the midst of loss, not prosperity."[18]

Larry King has interviewed Joel Osteen several times. On one occasion, King said to Joel "What if you're Jewish or Muslim and you don't accept Christ at all?" Osteen said "I'm very careful about saying who would and wouldn't go to heaven." King responds by asking "They're wrong, aren't they (referring to the Muslims and Jews)?" Osteen answers by saying "I don't know if I believe they're wrong." Osteen goes on to say "I've spent a lot of time in India with my father and I don't know all about their religion, but I know they love God....I've seen their sincerity."[19] Osteen fails to realize there is a huge chasm and discrepancy that exists between Christianity and Hinduism. For more information on some of the basic tenants of Hinduism, see the notes section for this chapter.[20]

I've also heard many people say that Muslims and Christians all worship the same God. It's incredibly difficult for me to understand how professed evangelicals can equate sincere and devoted Muslims who love Allah with professing Christians who love God. I can only conclude that we are not all talking about the same God.

Where is the line that Jesus so clearly drew in the sand when He said that He was *the* way, *the* truth and *the* life? Or when He claimed exclusivity with His Father? When Jesus said that *no one* gets to the Father except through Him, wasn't He drawing a pretty clear and divisive line in the sand? This was no imaginary line invented by radical Christian's centuries later. This line was drawn by Jesus Himself when He claimed His exclusive position as the only Mediator between God and man.[21] He also highlighted the existence of the line in the sand when He said that a prerequisite to saving our lives was losing them.[22]

Many Christians would like to make it appear as if God were neutral about all this and that Jesus just wants us all to get along and enjoy our best life now. But we know from searching the Word of God that this is simply not the case.

You don't have to look far on a given Sunday morning to hear someone behind a pulpit espousing tolerance and unity as the highest good, and teaching that you can have whatever you want if you simply dare to dream and believe. Neither would you have to look far to find a pastor delivering a passionate message with three points and a poem, with a closing plea to join him in repeating the sinner's prayer.

Here's the problem with that – it's just not what Jesus taught. Jesus taught that He held an exclusive ownership on people's lives. He taught that there would be many deceived people who would spend eternity separated from Him in a place of eternal destruction called hell. Jesus Himself taught that to truly follow Him meant dying to yourself. He espoused sacrificial living over indulgent living. He made it painfully clear that in order to follow Him we'd have to walk away from the enticing allures of the world. Jesus claimed that in order to know God, you had to know Him. By Jesus' own profession, He stated that it was impossible to have a relationship with God apart from knowing Him (Jesus) personally.

When we read the whole counsel of God, we do not have the liberty to walk away from those very difficult and costly claims that Jesus made. When we come to the cross, we abandon our rights and entitlements. We have been purchased at a high price, and our allegiance now belongs to our King. He has every right in the world to demand our attention, our affections, and the essence of our very lives. And our assessment of this shouldn't be an afterthought. It should be clearly and unapologetically taught to people who are contemplating the high cost of following Jesus.

We are guilty of having made an unbiblical distinction between the terms Savior and Lord. We boast about the grace and forgiveness that He's afforded our sinful souls, but do we boast the same confidence about His rightful place as Ruler of our lives and His authority to call us to a life of radical obedience? We seem ever so quick to tell people that the blood of Jesus purchased their pardon and allows them entrance into heaven. Are we as hasty to tell people that this same blood that redeems them also transfers ownership of their lives, which means they no longer belong to themselves? Are we intentional about telling people His position as Owner gives Him every right in the world to require that we walk away from everything to make His name great among the nations?

How is it that we've made peace with this unbiblical distinction between Savior and Lord? How have we become so accustomed to accepting for ourselves and offering to others the benefits of salvation while we completely ignore the costs? No, I'm not advocating we can earn our salvation. Not at all. We are saved by grace, through faith, and this is a gift from God, not something we can manufacture on our own. As such though, the Bible makes it clear that this particular saving faith that we're referring to, and a life of radical obedience to Jesus, are not mutually exclusive terms. They are in fact, mutually inclusive terms. They overlap to such a degree that you simply cannot have one without the other. When we separate the two, we render the gospel ineffective and further perpetuate this bogus heresy.

It's clear, the line has been drawn. Jesus stands at the entrance to eternity and arguably delivers a few of the most divisive statements in all of recorded history. He says, "If you love Me you will keep My commandments. Whoever has My commandments and keeps them, he it is who loves Me. If anyone loves Me, he will keep My word. Whoever does not love Me does not keep My words."[23]

There's the line. Did you see it? It may seem a bit vague at first glance. And that may just be because we've heard this so much that we've become somewhat desensitized to the depth of truth in these statements.

Jesus was clear; if we love Him, we will live according to His revealed Word. If we reject the truth revealed on the pages of Scripture and live contrary to the commands of Jesus, we simply cannot and do not love Him. Period. We can add a bunch of christianeze jargon onto it and package it up so it's less convicting for us and more palatable for unsuspecting passerbys, but it won't change the truth. The hard claims of Jesus make it clear that we are not all preaching and obeying the same gospel.

The time has come. We must rally around the cross and expose this heresy for what it is...a perverted religious program that offers benefits without cost, while systematically sending millions of unsuspecting people directly to a Christless eternity.

## OUR PRAYER

*Jesus, we stand guilty of looking for and embracing a gospel that You did not author. Our flesh longs for comfort and security. We gravitate towards those who coddle us and affirm us.*

*To agree with the truths we find in Your Word means we become not only enemies of the world but also enemies of many of those who profess to belong to You. We love the applause of men more than we love the glory of God and so we continually compromise our convictions.*

*Change our hearts, Lord Jesus. Take Your Word and use it to bring deep and lasting transformation to our lives. We long for what we do and what we say to bring pleasure to Your heart.*

*We know that Your will is that the nations would worship You as the rightful King of the universe and Lord over all. We gladly embrace Your purpose and plan to use us to take Your Word to the ends of the earth and to make disciples of all the nations. We* are humbled that You would sovereignly choose to incorporate us into Your redemptive plans for the world.

Thank You, Father, that regardless of the complacency and perversity that corrupts Your bride, we know that no purpose of Yours can be thwarted. We believe that You will sovereignly use the very evil and corruption that pollutes Your church to fulfill Your greatest redemptive purposes for all of the earth. Even so, purify us and make us a people who are committed to the purity of Your bride and who love Your glory more than we love ourselves.

It is with grateful hearts that we submit to Your authority and willfully choose to rally around Your throne to declare our allegiance to You. You alone are worthy. And for that, we love You and worship You.

May the Lamb receive the full reward of His suffering. Amen.

# 5

# NO MORE PATTY CAKE

## IF YOU CAN'T RUN WITH THE BIG DOGS, STAY ON THE PORCH

There's a company called Big Dogs that specialize in graphic tees. I remember seeing a shirt many years ago with the following line printed on the back: "If you can't run with the big dogs, stay on the porch." Well, I just Googled the Big Dogs company, and found a host of other similar shirts boasting the same type of theme. Here are a few:

> "If you can't run with the big dogs, stay in the pits."
> "If you can't hit with the big dogs, stay out of the park."
> "If you can't board with the big dogs, stay out of the
>   pipe."
> "If you can't run with the big dogs, stay off the field."
> "If you can't drive with the big dogs, stay on the range."

I'm certainly not promoting the Big Dogs brand. Many of their shirts carry with them a somewhat disguised, yet overt message saying something like: "I'm better than you and since you can't keep up with me, since you obviously don't play as well as me, since you can't drive as fast as me, just move aside." Or a similar message along those same lines.

The bottom line is they've branded a message that has struck a chord with many Americans. Right or wrong, it has. And as much as I disagree with this particular message, I believe we can certainly find a redemptive quality here to use for kingdom purposes. The walk away message from these shirts is simple — "I'm not playing patty-cake anymore." And this is a message we can certainly draw application from for our spiritual lives.

We would do well in our Christian teaching if we would help followers of Jesus or would-be followers of Jesus to understand that when someone decides to follow hard after Christ, they cease playing childish games. The days of Candy Land, Go Fish, Chutes and Ladders, and Patty Cake are over.

The ground rules for a passionate follower of Jesus Christ clearly haven't changed in over 2,000 years. Our understanding and interpretation of those ground rules needs to change though. And it needs to be a radical change. We can no longer carry the name "Christian" while living our lives as though Jesus were just some D-list movie star. While once we were comfortable coddling and cajoling people, we know that we can no longer take that approach. And even though there was a time when we were so afraid of offending someone that we became paralyzed in our efforts to proclaim the pure gospel, those days are long gone.

We've come to understand this call of Jesus on our lives is radical. It requires full submission and total dedication. To use a phrase from my Greek professor in college, we will no longer subscribe to a "limp wristed, mealy mouth, panty waste" version of the gospel. We will intentionally embrace the whole counsel of God, even the parts we are not comfortable with. We will choose to believe and obey all of Scripture, not just those verses and passages that sit well with us and cost us nothing. We will believe and obey, with equal fervor and passion, those very verses and passages that require the totality of our affections and the sum of our allegiance.

If you're still with me here and are interested in banning together to hold high the Word of God, the whole counsel of God, including all the difficult parts we conveniently tend to overlook and bypass, we must first tend to some sensitive and profoundly essential heart issues.

We would be foolish to think we can just walk away from the carnage we've taken part in creating. Certainly most of us would agree that over the years we've embraced and grown comfortable with a very shallow and skewed version of the gospel, which as we've already discussed is really no gospel at all. It is, in fact, a bogus, incomplete, distorted form of the gospel. But it is not the gospel. And in embracing this altered gospel, we've perpetuated this heresy and are therefore guilty of much of the spiritual carnage we see around us.

It would obviously be utterly foolish for either you or I to feel like we are entirely responsible for the spiritual decay we see across the board with Christianity in America. Even so, I must humbly acknowledge that for many years I've embraced an adulterated gospel. One that minimizes the gravity and weight of my sin, absolves me of my responsibility of living a radical life committed to the Great Commission, and ultimately cheapens the glory of God. In other words, we compromise the essence of the gospel while we routinely pimp out a cheapened version of the gospel marked only by grace and forgiveness and a fast pass to heaven. As painful as it is for me to admit, I stand guilty before God. For many years I have taken part in promoting, esteeming, and propagating this perverted gospel, which has indeed affected and influenced other people.

Before any of us can begin to move forward from here in picking up the baton of the whole counsel of God and affirming the truths and mandates we find in it, we must first confess our nasty sin and repent of our corrupt and maligned thinking. I want to encourage you to take some time now to lay your soul bare before the throne of God. Confess your sin. Take some time to repent – not just turning *from* some jacked up thinking, but turning *to* God's pure, unadulterated Word. I'll lead us in a prayer together at the end of this chapter. I challenge you to join me in making this prayer and petition the cry of your heart.

Part of walking away from childish games and embracing this radical life God has called us to, is getting serious about the very things that God is serious about. We know with great certainty that He takes seriously His commands to us to be and make disciples. Clearly He is serious when He commands that our love for Him must be greater, deeper, and carry more weight than the love we have for ourselves, other people, and the idols in this life we've grown so fond of and attached to.

If we conclude from Scripture that God is most definitely sober-minded about His plan to use the gospel to reach and teach the world, then we must also become sober-minded about radical, Biblical, God-honoring, Christ-exalting discipleship. As we are discovering, discipleship is the primary means that God has chosen to use to raise up a vast multitude of worshippers from every tribe and tongue and people and nation who are wholly committed to peculiar and perpetual obedience. More on this in later chapters.

For now though, we must first start with an honest assessment of our sin and wickedness. Why? Why should we spend time dwelling on our sin and our jacked up theology? Simply put – we should get serious about our sin because God is serious about our sin and He calls us to repent. Actually He commands us to repent. Below are a few of the verses that address Scriptures clear mandate to repent and our dire need to repent:

- **Matthew 4.17** *"From that time on Jesus began to preach, 'Repent, for the kingdom of heaven has come near.'"* (NIV)
- **Luke 15.7** *"Just so, I tell you, there will be more joy in heaven over one sinner who repents than over ninety-nine righteous persons who need no repentance."*
- **Acts 3.19** *"Repent, then, and turn to God, so that your sins may be wiped out, that times of refreshing may come from the Lord..."* (NIV)

- **Acts 17.30** *"In the past God overlooked such ignorance, but now He commands all people everywhere to repent."* (NIV)
- **Romans 2.4** *"Or do you presume on the riches of His kindness and forbearance and patience, not knowing that God's kindness is meant to lead you to repentance?"*
- **Revelation 3.19** *"Those whom I love I rebuke and discipline. So be earnest and repent."* (NIV)

It's clear, repentance is as necessary for our spiritual lives as oxygen is for our physical lives. And repentance begins when our hearts and our minds have a collision with the penetrating truth found in God's Word. According to Romans 12, our lives are transformed as our minds are renewed and our thinking changes. And a byproduct of that happening in our lives is proven by our desire to walk before the Lord with pure and upright hearts. It is imperative that our theology - those Biblical beliefs and convictions we build our lives on - is solid so that we can be intentional and obedient as we live the lives God has called us to live.

Far too many of us and our churches stand guilty before God for a myriad of different reasons. And it seems most would prefer to keep ourselves and our churches busy, focus on the positive, and neglect the rare discipline of corporate confession and repentance.

We are severely deluded if we think God just turns a blind eye to our sin and unfaithfulness. Our theology is soiled and corrupt if we presume God simply sweeps our petty sin under the carpet. Let's remind ourselves that no sin is petty. All sin carries a significant stench and plays an equal part in the world's need for redemption. The sin of murder and the sin of pride are equally as revolting to God. Sure, degrees of sin carry different consequences. But we should be clear that sin is sin. The sin of whatever lands men and women behind bars is no different from the sin that you and I commit on a daily basis. We each stand equally guilty before a holy God.

I celebrate the fact that the finished work of Christ is the only thing that allows anyone to stand forgiven before God. And as genuine believers in Christ, we do indeed stand innocent before God because of the shed blood of Christ. Our sins have been atoned for and our hearts have been made new because of Jesus' obedience to the Father in laying down His life for the sins of mankind, and that includes me and you.

If our sin has already been forgiven, then what's the problem? Why do we need to spend any more time confessing and repenting? Why must we rehash our failings and shortcomings? In part, because they are not failings and shortcomings as we like to call them. They are sin. Plain and simple.

Here's the problem - when we sin, our sin breaks our fellowship with God until we confess it and repent of it. Although God sees us as holy through His Son, the Lord Jesus Christ, we are still in need of confessing our sins as a means to repair the fracture our sin has created in our fellowship with God. Our sin can also cause our prayers to fall on deaf ears in the corridors of heaven. King David made it clear that when we have known, unconfessed sin in our lives, God chooses not to hear our prayers.[1]

Arrogance abounds when we continue in sin with little or no thought of regular confession and repentance. We are spiritually anemic if our lives are not marked by these two essential disciplines. And it appears that far too many churches today have attempted to take the easy way out. They might occasionally make course corrections along the way but seldom take the necessary time to renounce, both privately and corporately, their skewed, perverted theology and grievous sin.

We most definitely need personal confession and repentance. We also need corporate confession and repentance. Church leaders need to invest time in helping their people see how we've embraced bad doctrine and warped theology over the years and how this grieves the heart of God. Pastors also need to help their people see how our skewed interpretations of Scripture have altered our view of God's glory, the need for His mercy, the extent of His grace, the magnitude of His self-sufficiency, His fundamental commands to take up our cross and follow Him, and the implications of a God whose plans will not and cannot be thwarted. (For a few introductory verses about man's inability to thwart God's sovereign purposes, check out Job 42.2, Isaiah 46.9-11, and Daniel 4.35).

You can spend time on your own before God asking the Holy Spirit to bring conviction to your heart and make you painfully aware of what you may have done to grieve the heart of the Father. I'd make a list if I were you. Write these things down. Take whatever time is necessary to get serious about your sin. God is serious about it and wants us to be too. Once you've written them down, spend time going through each one of the things you listed to confess and repent of them. Seeing your sin on paper and hearing yourself name it will certainly help you understand the gravity and weight of your sin. In understanding the weight and grievous nature of our sin, we will understand even more fully the magnitude of the grace and mercy of God. He who has been forgiven little loves little. But he who has been forgiven much loves much. The more we acknowledge and understand how massive our sin really is, and how extravagant the grace and forgiveness of God really is, the more extravagant our love for God and for His glory will be. And subsequently the more eager we will be to give the whole of our lives away to make His name great among the nations.[2]

## OUR PRAYER

*I have seen You in the sanctuary and beheld Your power and Your glory, and because Your love is better than life, my lips will praise You. I will praise You as long as I live and in Your name I will lift up my hands. My soul will be satisfied as with the richest of foods.*

*You are God and You alone stand worthy of our worship. You alone cause the sun to rise and the sun to set. By the power of Your word, You created each of the hundreds of trillions of stars* and then flung them into space. You even know their names. You created the wind and the waves and hold the keys to life and death. Not a single snowflake or drop of rain falls from the sky without Your knowledge.

Salvation belongs to only You and You will be faithful to save Your elect. You have sovereignly purposed to use Your people in Your plan to redeem the world and we are awed by that. We stand humbled before You that You would choose to redeem our lives, pull us from the mire and muck of our own pathetic lives, set our feet on rock solid ground, mercifully reconcile us to Yourself, and then make us faithful ambassadors of Your message of reconciliation. We are indeed Your ambassadors, so please supernaturally empower us to live as such.

For years You have patiently endured our foolish pride and arrogance. It is true, over the years, we've adopted and embraced only part of Your gospel. And in embracing only part of Your Word, we have nullified the entirety of it. By not accepting and embracing the whole counsel of God, we've fabricated an entirely new gospel, which is really no gospel at all. We have not personally embraced the hard claims of Jesus and are therefore unable to beckon others to abandon the totality of their lives for the cause of Christ and the glory of Your name.

Our hearts have been deceived. Our eyes have been blinded. Our ears are often deaf to hear Your voice. Jesus, You said that Your sheep hear Your voice. You know them and they follow You.

*If we really are Your sheep, teach us to recognize Your voice above the voices of the world. We are bombarded by lesser gods vying for our allegiance. Instead of drowning out all the competing voices we hear, teach us to willfully treasure You, love You, and choose You above these other gods.*

*We stand guilty before You of embracing and perpetuating a horribly perverted form of the gospel. We have set aside the costly endeavor of following Jesus and instead have encouraged people to look to You as Savior with little or no thought of explaining to them that You are first and foremost Lord. And as Lord, You have demanded that we repent and come to You. Your call is not a benign, safe, alluring invitation to come and find security. Rather, Your call is a dangerous one to lose our very lives. You've beckoned us to come and die, take up Your cross, render ourselves dead, crucify our flesh, and commit our lives to making much of Your name and renown in the world. We confess we have disregarded Your radical call to follow You and have forfeited our pursuit of You as the Treasure of our lives.*

*We know You are able, so for our good and for Your glory, would You purge our hearts of anything and everything that would compete for our total alliance to You? Because of Your great kindness, would You lead us to repentance? And because You do all things well, would You please continue to conform our hearts and transform our lives to the image of Jesus?*

*We confess to You and You alone that we stand before You guilty. We've elevated gift above Giver. We've elevated health above the Physician. We've elevated full bellies above hungry hearts. We have indeed cheapened Your glory and grace by ignoring the depth and magnitude of our own filthy sin. When we ignore our sin, we presume our innocence and minimize the vast expanse of Your mercies that are new every morning.*

*Forgive us, God, for all the years we've spent embracing a cheapened version of the gospel while minimizing the high cost of following Jesus. We've traded what it means to give our lives away for Your name and renown, in order to secure our seat in Your eternal kingdom. We've wrongly assumed that praying a prayer to escape the tortures of hell is the same as embracing a life devoted to the high cost of following Jesus.*

*You've made it clear in Your Word that what we have doesn't belong to us. You are the rightful Owner of it and You've loaned it to us, with the expectation that we will steward it well and invest it in building Your kingdom. O God, we must confess that we've hoarded our material possessions and we've not learned to give sacrificially. We've given out of our excess, with very little or no cost involved, and then asked You to bless it. We hold a death grip on our 401(k)'s, retirement packages, and our plans for a secure future, while consistently passing up opportunities to meet the dire needs of those around us. What a mockery we've made of what it means to be a radical disciple of Jesus Christ and an extravagant giver of all that You've given us to steward.*

*We know that You are indeed most glorified in us when we are most satisfied in You. We confess that we've embraced a distorted gospel which teaches us to look for Your handouts instead of looking for You. We've wrongly assumed that You are somehow appeased when we are busy playing church. Instead of learning how to treasure You above all else, we've learned to seek after and treasure the things You give us and the things You do for us.*

*Because our souls are not satisfied in Christ alone, our hearts go in silent search of other lovers. Forgive us, Lord, for being adulterers. We have indeed embraced other lovers along the way. At times we've been discontent with You and attempted to fill our hearts with the affections and pleasures of pathetic substitutes.*

*You've warned us that You are indeed a jealous God and that You do not share Your glory. We stand guilty of ever so subtly attempting to overthrow the glory that belongs to You and take it captive for ourselves.*

*We confess our heinous sins before You with a full understanding that our sin grieves Your heart. We know our sin is not small, as we like to think. We agree with the writer of Hebrews that nothing is hidden from Your sight. You see our nasty sin, You see our attempts to hide, and You are fully aware of the depth of our brokenness.*

*Thank You, God, for Your glory. Thank You, Father, for Your mercy. We bless You because Your grace is sufficient. We are enamored by the wisdom and the beauty that You behold.*

*We long to be faithful to the high calling we have to be sons and daughters of the King. Help us to faithfully represent You well to the world. May our message be pure. May our hearts be ignited. And may the totality of our lives be spent preaching the gospel to the world and making radical, passionate, God-honoring, Christ-exalting disciples of all the nations.*

*We love You and are grateful that You choose to love us. Through Jesus we pray, Amen.*

# GOING FOR BROKE

## IT'S AN ALL OR NOTHING PROPOSITION

For far too long we've treated Christianity like a classic sales pitch. We focus all of our time on the benefits with little or no conscious thought of the costs involved. As a suave saleswoman shifts our attention to the features and benefits of her product, she likewise is cleverly diverting our attention away from what purchasing her product will cost us.

And in a very similar fashion, are we not all guilty of doing the same thing? Aren't we much like a seasoned salesperson? We focus people's attention on the obvious benefits of having a relationship with God and spend little or no time talking about the high cost of following Jesus.

Think about it. If we told people up front that following Jesus could potentially cost them their lives, how many would still want to sign up? If we made it clear that Jesus was not simply an escape from the tortures of hell, but He was the Lord of the universe who would demand their very lives, how many would still willfully and gladly choose to follow Him?

We must be straight with people up front. Jesus is not an afterthought. He is not some wimpy little Savior standing at your front door begging you to follow Him. He isn't whimpering over in the corner like a cowering dog looking for a little affection. He is the King of the world, the Master of the universe, the Creator of all that is and the Lord over all of His creation, the Redeemer of all mankind, the Mighty God who holds the keys to life and death, and the Sovereign Lord who works all things according to the counsel of His will.

And as such He demands that He reside on the throne of our hearts. He is not content playing second fiddle to some puny lesser gods nor is He appeased as we give Him our leftovers. He demands that He alone be the object of our affections and the focus of our attention.

Does it make you uncomfortable to think that God is demanding? If so, I'd like to encourage you to read John Piper's book *What Jesus Demands From The World*. It will help you see clearly that there are a host of things that Jesus does indeed make demands about.

We can no longer treat our relationship with God as secondary. If we indeed *have* a relationship with God in Christ, it must take center stage. He demands every crack and crevice of our lives. He demands our worship. He makes certain and specific demands on our attention and our affections.

As a committed follower of Jesus Christ, it is clear we can no longer continue to warm the pews. We cannot continue playing "church" on Sunday mornings, while that day remains disconnected from the other six days of the week for us. It will no longer suffice to check church attendance off our "to do" list each week, as if we're somehow meriting God's favor for that particular week by jumping through the necessary hoop to secure it. We will no longer sit idly by as others around us take seriously God's mandate to take the gospel to the whole world and make disciples of all the nations.

Listen, if your greatest concern on Sunday morning is getting out in time to get somewhere good for lunch without having to wait in line, then we're probably on two different pages here. If you sit in church like the ref at a track meet who's primarily concerned with the "time," then it's quite probable that you need to hear this - following Jesus really is an all or nothing proposition.

Perhaps some of you have a pile of 'how to' books lining your book shelves. It's not my intent to write another one of those books. For a few nanoseconds on the spectrum of eternity I simply want to shine the spotlight on Biblical discipleship and ask God to bring the necessary conviction and obedience, so we respond appropriately and join a peculiar band of passionate followers of Jesus Christ scattered around this giant globe we live on. It should be our deepest hearts desire that at some point in the near future, all of us will gladly join in to be an active part of God's master plan to make disciples of all the nations of the world.

I'm not a gambler and never have been. But sadly, I've watched enough TV to know what a casino looks like and I have a pretty good idea of how one would place a wager.

First, you decide how much you'd like to bet. Next, you lay down your chips. And finally, you wait in anticipation as the cards are played or the dice are rolled. Some people no doubt play conservatively, using only a small percentage of the total amount of chips they hold. Others may tend to be a bit more adventurous and occasionally even risk it all. That's when the phrase "go for broke" get's thrown out there. "Go for broke" is an informal idiom and means: to commit or expend all of one's available resources toward achievement of a goal. As the phrase implies, going for broke really is an all or nothing proposition.

As followers of Jesus, He's called each one of us to go for broke. He never calls anyone to play conservatively. He didn't then, and He doesn't now. Of course, we've been conditioned to believe that God is conservative and that He certainly wouldn't want you to risk your life to follow Him. And because many of us have personalities that tend to be marked by structure, planning, and playing it safe, we assume God wants us to stay that way.

However, Scripture speaks of a different kind of life for those who choose to align themselves with this man, Jesus Christ. Time after time in both the Old and New Testaments, God requires full submission and total abandonment. Playing it safe isn't a viable option simply because it is completely antithetical to virtually everything that marks a devoted follower of the Jesus in the Bible.

We don't have to look too far through the pages of Scripture to see a common theme here. Think with me of the story of Abraham. God called him to slaughter his son. How about Noah? God called him to invest one hundred years of his life building a boat, before anyone knew what rain was. How about Nehemiah? Anyone up for the monumental task of rebuilding the walls around Jerusalem? Remember Esther? In her quest to go for broke she was willing to risk losing her head. What about the conspicuous apostle Paul? Though once a former antagonist towards Christians, he exhausted his new, regenerated life going for broke. He literally risked it all, on a daily basis, to spread a passion for the supremacy of God. The disciples each walked away from the lives they were comfortable with in order to respond to the call of Jesus to come and follow Him. And as I've already mentioned, each of these men, with the exception of John, lost their lives in a horribly brutal fashion.

So what do we make of all this? Should we conclude that going for broke is something only "called" people would consider doing? Do we assume it's just the crazy, radical people who would risk their lives for the sake of the gospel? Does God really call all of us to be willing to risk our lives for the cause of Christ? Yes, yes and yes!

We have indeed been called by the God of the universe. In the eyes of the world we will certainly appear crazy. And like it or not, living the life we've been called to will no doubt include some ginormous risks that will likely appear irresponsible and insane to those around us.

As we consider the roll of a committed follower of Jesus Christ, may I ask you a simple question? How can someone be redeemed by the Creator and Redeemer of the universe and not turn a bit fanatical? Is it possible to have the living God take up residence in our hearts in the form of the Holy Spirit, without some drastic changes taking place in our personality, character and modus operandi for living life? If we've accepted the call to follow Jesus, aren't we in fact the "called" ones? And isn't going for broke something each one of us should intentionally purpose to do with whatever years or months or days we have remaining on this planet?

Imagine the honor that God would receive and the impact we could potentially have on the kingdom of God if we'd rise from the ashes of complacency and mediocrity and put on the robe of abandonment. I'm not talking about joining a church group or signing up for another conference. I'm talking about realigning our lives so our affections and our loyalties are given to the One to Whom they are due. I'm talking about stepping out of the normative life of a casual observer or comfortable bystander and accepting the call of Jesus to abandon all and follow hard after Him. After all, Jesus isn't simply looking for loyal fans to support His team, He's looking for committed followers who are willing to lose it all for His cause.

Each one of us, without exception, should purpose to live lives of radical, God-honoring, Christ-exalting, purposeful obedience. We have one life to live and it would be a tragedy if we wasted it by attempting to follow Jesus while living a safe, predictable, secure, and mediocre life.

Thinking of all the people who will unfortunately waste their lives reminds me of the guy who spent his whole life climbing a ladder. He spent his days, year after year, tirelessly climbing the rungs of this ladder. When it was all said and done and the man got to the top of his ladder he was completely and utterly devastated. He made the painful realization that his ladder was up against the wrong wall. What a tragedy to know that he spent all of those years and exhausted all of that effort climbing for nothing.

And what a similar tragedy it is to watch people wasting their lives before your very eyes. You know them. I know them. Perhaps you even feel like one of those people right now. It is indeed a monumental calamity to see people waste their lives on trivial pursuits that have no lasting significance. But Scripture is clear, it doesn't have to be that way. You have not been sentenced to waste your life. No matter the plight of your past, you are not defined by what you've done or by what's been done to you. Today is a new day and you can courageously choose to invest the rest of your life for the cause of Christ as opposed to squandering your remaining days and wasting it all.

In an effort to paint a picture of what it might look like to jump in head first and live a life of radical obedience, I'd like to share a few of my journal and blog entries. Perhaps reading a few, random blurbs about following Jesus will help connect some dots for you and put into clearer perspective what it looks like for an average, ordinary person (like me!) to live for God's name and renown. And perhaps it might just debunk the myth that radical discipleship is reserved for the "professionals."

As a bit of a disclaimer I want you to know these journal and blog entries were not written with this book in mind. In other words, I wasn't writing them with the intent to ever have them published. The journals were written and filed. Until now, they've never been read by anyone. And the blog entries were simply written for the purpose of posting on my blog. They may seem a bit random. And they are. I picked some I thought would help give you a glimpse of what it might look like to live an intentional life, out of the box, with a view of eternity in mind. (The blog entries have titles; the journal entries simply have dates.)

# PERSECUTION WITH A PURPOSE

It's been twenty two years since God sovereignly pulled me out of the muck and mire of my world, drew me to Himself, and gave me a new heart. Someday I'd like to write a book about this journey. Not because my story is anything grand. It's really not. My story, like yours, is really just a demonstration of the sovereignty and grace of God. And that's the part I'd like to make much about.

For twenty years I've sat under a variety of different pastors and have of course, listened and learned from many others as well. I'm grateful for technology that enables me to listen to, read, and watch guys that I'd otherwise never have a chance to meet in person. My view and understanding of God, my love for Him and His word, and my effectiveness in ministry have all been greatly enhanced because of the advances in modern technology over the past ten years.

Lately though, I've become increasingly critical of those I suspect have a warped theology, bad doctrine, and propagate a false gospel. Call me a cynic. Call me judgmental. Call me what you want. I'm just being honest. I'm certainly not setting myself up as judge and jury. At least that's not my intent. I'm simply making assessments based on what I see, hear, and read. I believe we're all called to do that. And certainly the Light of Christ has enabled us and equipped us with His Spirit to help ensure we aren't led away by false teachers and don't follow savage wolves (dressed as sheep).

Truth be told, I was recently accused of being a savage wolf. Yep, I'm not kidding. There are a few guys in Oklahoma who have taken their stand against me. Guys I don't really even know. We're more acquaintances than anything. I've spent a cumulative total of about 20 hours with them as we attempted to partner together with an outreach event in Liberia, Africa. In any event though, they called me the other day to let me know they've determined I'm a wolf in sheep's clothing. They're peeved because I wasn't willing to embrace the easy believism, prosperity gospel they were trying to peddle in Liberia. I boldly spoke against it and speaking against their message was in essence speaking against them. And for that, they've pegged me as the wolf, which frankly, I can live with.

Maybe you're nodding your head back and forth in disbelief. I find myself doing that as well from time to time. It's disheartening for me to believe that so called "Christians" can and do act like this. All in the name of Christianity. I'm not surprised so many unregenerate people are turned off by what they see in churches across America, because more often than not they don't see a significant difference between the world and American Christianity. And let's be honest, there really isn't a difference between the world and American Christianity. If a difference truly exists, it's so nominal, one would hardly even notice.

It certainly isn't my intent to hash out my monumental disagreements here against these Oklahoma dudes. After talking with each of them at length about our 'differences,' I believe the most profitable thing I can do is disengage from any further dialogue with them and pray that God accomplishes His redemptive purposes in their lives. As I've told each one of them, I love them and don't harbor any hatred towards them. I sincerely pray God changes their hearts.

As this ordeal with these Oklahoma guys has unfolded, I've come face to face with the realities of the content contained in First Peter. As it is, our church is preaching through First Peter right now, so I've been trying to absorb myself in this book each day - asking God to wash my heart and my mind with the Truth of His Word. I trust it's working.

Peter talks a great deal about persecution. The kind of persecution that could cause you to lose your head. Literally. I don't think he's talking about the kind of persecution you might get if you were to wear your Christian t-shirt to work or to school and have to endure a bit of snickering from a few of your peers. Or the kind of persecution you might face if you were caught reading your Bible on your lunch break. Or perhaps even the type of persecution you might receive from your friends because you've decided you're telling your kids up front that there is no Santa Claus. I don't even think Peter's talking about the kind of persecution you receive when you take your firm stand against the putrid prosperity gospel and those who propagate it.

No, no, no. Peter is not referring to *that* kind of persecution. We're talking persecution for living a righteous, holy, upright, uncompromising life, committed to the Lordship of Jesus. A life that unashamedly proclaims the hard truth of the gospel, even in the face of certain ridicule and persecution. The people Peter was writing to were just those kinds of people. They were facing certain hardships and persecution from the Romans and pagans around them. Following Jesus wasn't popular. And often times it led to certain death. Peter's expressed purpose in writing his epistle was that his readers would stand firm in the true grace of God[1] in the face of escalating persecution and suffering. Peter wanted his readers to live triumphantly in the midst of hostility without abandoning hope, becoming bitter, losing faith in Christ, or forgetting Christ's second coming. He wanted his readers to know that when they are obedient to God's Word despite the world's antagonism, Christians' lives will testify to the truth of the gospel.[2]

I'm certainly not facing this type of persecution. I doubt you are either. Unless you're reading this from someplace like a cold prison cell in China or a remote jungle in Peru. My guess is the persecution you face is much like the persecution I face. Hardly worthy of even calling persecution. I suppose in some small way it might resemble persecution, but certainly not indicative of the type of intense, severe, life-threatening persecution Peter is referring to.

My prayer has increasingly been that I would gladly welcome trials and hardships. That I would learn to accept and embrace persecution. Real persecution. The kind of persecution and suffering that develops perseverance and ultimately proves the reality of my faith. I long to treasure the infinite value and worth of Jesus more than anything else, and I'm realizing this most likely isn't going to happen just because I'm a pastor or because I read my Bible and have a few verses memorized. This will only happen as I'm faced with the hard realities of choosing Jesus over my idols. And it will happen as I'm forced to heed Christ's radical call on my life as opposed to walking comfortably through the wide gate and taking the broad road that many others seem to be choosing.

The more I learn the Word of God, the more convinced I am that God chose me in Him before the foundations of the world, that I might fearlessly declare the glories of the Exalted One. This humbles me and provides ample motivation to abandon my life for the sake of His call. And it should you too.

# THURSDAY - 4.29.2010

A great morning. Have felt rather cold for the past few months. Pockets of closeness to God, but nothing consistent. Not sure why I'd wander, but it seems my heart has grown cold. And I have continually ignored it. Until this morning. My heart hurts over how quick I can pursue other gods and how comfortable I become settling for crumbs off the floor. Forgive me Lord for my waywardness and hardheartedness. I am repulsed by both.

Sharing this morning with some students about Cross Cultural Ministry has forced me to be in the Word, a place I haven't consistently been in quite some time. I'm embarrassed that I seem to have embraced this level of complacency and mediocrity over the past few weeks.

Plant Your Word deep in me, Lord, and make me hunger and thirst for Your righteousness. Forgive me for having pitiful faith. Teach me to believe You and take You at Your Word. Please make me effective in peoples' lives. I want to waste my life on kingdom things.

I'm reading a bit of Jim Elliot's journal entries. I'm inspired, encouraged, challenged, and humbled by his mark on modern day Christianity. He was an amazing example of a committed follower of Christ, laying down his life for the sake of the gospel and willing to risk it all. May I be willing to do the same.

## KARAOKE AND JESUS

Last night was an interesting night. Partly depressing. Partly convicting. Partly enlightening. Let me try to explain.

I've been in Ohio this past week taking care of some family issues. While here, I'm trying to make good use of my time. When I'm not working on the issues that brought me here, I'm trying to invest my time with some other extended family that I unfortunately don't see often enough.

My cousin Wendy and her husband Steve own a steak house in Twin Lakes, Ohio, called the Rusty Nail. Wendy is a recovering addict. She was bad off. Really bad off. Ten years on the streets using and abusing drugs and alcohol. During the most critical time of her years on drugs, months would go by without anyone knowing if she were dead or alive. Needless to say, those were ten excruciatingly long, painful months for her family.

One evening Wendy and I enjoyed a meal together at her restaurant and had a great time talking. Our conversation soon turned to spiritual things as we talked late into the night. My cousin Wendy is my age, and I'm ashamed to admit that I've never sat down and had a significant conversation with her. But it happened this week and it marked me. During our talk, she said "I really need to get to know this Jesus and learn more about Him." And she didn't say this because I prompted her to. This was simply an obvious demonstration that God was indeed working in her life.

Tonight, my mom and I went back out to my cousin's restaurant to have dinner and to give Wendy a few books I had purchased for her. In addition to a couple short Piper books, I gave her a Couples Bible and the book *Radical* by David Platt. Both of which I believe will be instrumental in her life as she gets to know the Jesus of the Bible and discovers His redemptive and salvific plan for her life and His radical call for her to abandon her life for His cause. I can't wait to see all this unfold.

My mom and I sat in the bar area and enjoyed a great meal. It's Friday night and Friday night at The Rusty Nail is Karaoke Night. We watched for an hour and a half as aspiring singers gave their all. Some were able to carry a note, while others, well let's just say, they should stick to their day jobs. The last time I sat through Karaoke was back in the late 80's and truthfully, I was not sober enough that night to remember much of it. This night was different. I was one hundred percent sober, lucid and had all my faculties together.

I've been labeled a professional people watcher. And I understand people watching is not a spiritual gift. Even so, I enjoy it and it's often a great way to pass the time.

As people watching goes, tonight was no exception. There were plenty of interesting people to watch and listen to. As I sat watching and taking in all that I was seeing, my heart began to break. My heart broke as I watched people sit at the bar and drink. And then I started adding up all the money they were spending on their alcohol. It's significant. Very significant. It didn't take long before I was thinking of all the desperately needy kids in Africa we could feed and care for with this money.

It really was depressing. Incredibly disheartening to watch all these people waste so much of their time and money sitting at a bar. Some were single, others were couples. In either case many were just looking for something to ease the pain, minimize the stress, and allow them to enjoy an evening uninhibited by the realities of the daily grind of life.

I also left tonight feeling enlightened and convicted. I was reminded that by and large, I was surrounded by lost people. Not judging, just making an educated assessment. Certainly these are not the people that have the abundant life that Jesus came to bring us. These are not the people who are enthralled by the glory of Jesus. This bar didn't seem to be occupied by people who have experienced the reality and depth of the grace of God.

And I was struck by this not-so-deep-but-eternally-significant thought. If this is the place where people who are estranged from God hang out, why wouldn't I spend more time hanging out in places like this? Why are my days filled with safe places and safe, relatively clean people? Why don't I make more of an effort to go places where Jesus would go and hang out with the kind of people that Jesus would (and did!) hang out with?

You might remember Jesus went to a wedding in John 2. Not only were they serving alcohol, but Jesus Himself made wine. His first recorded miracle was turning water into wine, right there at the wedding.

In John 4 we read about Jesus intentionally walking through the town of Samaria, which was a definite no-no for Jews. And to top it off, He actually even talked to a woman there. A double no-no! In John 8 we read about His interaction with the adulteress brought before Him for stoning. Perhaps in our culture, we would avoid this situation all-together. After all, being seen with a known hooker or promiscuous woman could seriously destroy our professional and personal reputation.

In Matthew 8 and Mark 1 we read about Jesus' interaction with lepers. That doesn't mean much to us in our culture, but perhaps hanging out with a leper back then would be the equivalent to hanging out with someone carrying around a deadly virus today. Lepers were banned from town and were

140

by and large banned from interaction with the general population. Being seen with a leper wasn't exactly what you did to win friends and influence people. And in both Mark 3 and Luke 6, we read the account of Jesus healing a guy with a jacked up hand...on the Sabbath! Again, a religious and cultural taboo.

In Luke 5 Scripture says Jesus invited a tax collector named Levi to join His small band of followers. Tax collectors were not the most popular or liked guys around. Jesus once again showed His defiance for hollow and hypocritical religion void of eternal truth and authentic compassion.

The reality is our cushy, conservative, American churches frown upon church members frequenting bars and pubs. They most certainly don't encourage pastors to spend time in those establishments either. Our plan is – let the lost, spiritually estranged, hell bound sinners come to us. Let's spend all of our time and invest all of our resources on our big buildings and fancy "outreach" ministries and hope that our buildings will be attractive enough to woo the lost people to come to us.

But for the love of God, we shouldn't go to those shady places where other church members might happen to see us enter or recognize our car parked out front, wrongly identify us as one of those 'sinners' and start the holy huddle rumors that we've taken a hard fall from grace.

So, tonight I had a revelation. Wanna know what it was? It is simply this - I need to get my butt off the pew and plop it down on a bar stool. And I need to do that often. Intentionally. Decisively. With great compassion and with a clear conviction that Jesus has indeed called me to infiltrate the darkness. He didn't call me to ask the darkness to find my light. He has commanded me to take His light into the dark places of this earth.

Will you join me in abandoning all the foolish and naïve manmade church rules we tend to hide behind in an effort to escape the clear command from Jesus to go into all the world? Will you join me in getting radical and vigilant by spending our days impacting the darkness instead of continuing to waste our resources trying to get lost people to find us? We've wasted far too much of our time and resources with that approach. Let's model Jesus' approach and go places where lost people are.

Keep in mind that Jesus Himself has called us to abandon our lives for the sake of the gospel. So unless your underage or alcohol is a temptation of yours, I'd suggest you go find a local pub, pick up a microphone and join the karaoke. I'm convinced these are the people that Jesus referred to as 'harassed and helpless, like sheep without a shepherd.' Will we continue to drive by these types of establishments and pray for them to come find us, or will we begin praying that God would break our hearts for lost and hurting people so much so that we are compelled to engage people the way Jesus would?

*This blog entry above was written in early December of 2010. Last night, December 27, 2010 a youth pastor friend of mine from North Dakota came to Asheville to visit. We had a great dinner and enjoyed several hours of encouraging conversation. After dinner, we visited a local pub. About thirty minutes into our time there, we noticed a few Bible's sitting on shelves high above the bar. My friend asked our server if she knew why they were there. She had no idea. After a series of seemingly benign follow up questions, we started asking our server what she thought about religion, God, the Bible, etc. She seemed genuinely excited and eager to talk about her faith journey. She said she comes from a long line of Southern Baptists but claimed to be an agnostic herself. She just wasn't sure about it all and didn't want to say she was 'into' something without having more information about it.

Our servers name was Trish. I assured her I'd be back and we'd continue our conversation. Trish is not someone who would show up to your average church on Sunday morning. But she is certainly someone who would be willing to sit in her pub, surrounded by a bunch of drinkers, and share her heart about God, the Bible, her struggles with her faith, etc, etc. As you might imagine, I'm looking forward to my next trip to the pub.

# MONDAY - 7.27.09

Thank You, God, for Your faithfulness and mercy. Without both, I'd be instantly taken to hell where I'd suffer for all of eternity. I know I deserve that, but You've chosen to redeem me and give me life. I really pray that I'd live my life so that my obedience to You proves my gratefulness and love for You.

The past few weeks have been amazing. I feel like I'm learning so much from my time in Your Word. 1 Peter has been challenging. Teaching/preaching through it has been super beneficial. And I've been encouraged to see how You're working in people's hearts and lives. Some have shared with me what You are teaching them and I stand amazed. Thanks for letting me be a small part of what You're doing to change people's view of You and their response to You. What You're doing with Mike B is totally amazing. Thank You for that.

There's so much on my heart about my job. But, I'm totally trusting that You sovereignly brought us to this place and You will be faithful to fulfill Your purposes in us and through us. Teach me how to be patient as I wait. Teach me how to be focused as I fix my eyes on Jesus. Teach me obedience from my suffering. I know my suffering isn't really suffering at all. As Jesus learned obedience from what He suffered, please use the painful things in my own life to teach me obedience too.

Saturday was really cool. I spent some time with Ryan. He's wrestling with some great stuff. Great in the sense that they are issues that can potentially lead to great maturity in his life and will also help equip him for whatever You've called him to.

He texted a few things that totally blew my mind. Phrased some things that sounded more mature than most adults I know. I was encouraged and challenged by that. I also realized that if You chose to bring our family to this town just so that I could witness the work You're doing in Ryan's life, it would have been worth it. I trust there are other reasons we're here, but even if there aren't, I'm honored and humbled to watch from the sidelines how You're changing his heart and helping him to wrestle with things that will help shape him into the man that You've called him to be.

Saturday he and I talked some about discipleship. If he truly pursues it, he'll be in a boat with only a few others. I think he's at a critical point where he'll either break from the crowd and become a passionate, radical, lover of Jesus or he'll blend in with the rest of the 'Christian' kids who seem to be plagued with mediocrity and complacency. Don't let him settle for that. I offered to spend time with him each week discipling him. I hope he takes me up on it...for several reasons. Set him apart God. Call him to something so far beyond himself that he'd know without question that it's from You.

I love you, Jesus. Thanks for loving me. Help me to live this week like it's my last week on earth. Saturate my influence and effectiveness so that Your kingdom is expanded and Your name and renown become the desire of people's hearts. I pray this for Your names sake.

## HERE'S WHAT I'M LEARNING, STRUGGLING WITH, REALIZING...

My good friend Jody Kidd emailed me today and asked me what I've been learning. Here was my answer to him.

- I'm often times a big jerk.
- My flesh is hungry for sin. Hungrier than I care to admit.
- God's love for me is staggering. The depths of which I cannot grasp.
- There are a lot of really messed up people around me who are hurting beyond comprehension.
- Christians can be really stupid and annoying.

145

- I'm often uncomfortable telling people I'm a "Christian". I just like to tell them I'm striving to be a radical follower of Jesus.
- Often times I'm privately hyper-critical of "Christians" who have a lot of fancy, expensive, excessive stuff. It's hard for me to reconcile a radical gospel with a comfortable lifestyle.
- I say I love God but often times the last thing on my 'to do' list is reading His Word.
- My heart aches for people who are suffering in Africa.
- Political people who put their own twisted, selfish interests above the needs of those they are serving, shouldn't be in office.
- I've read a bunch of hateful blogs and emails this week from professed "Christians." All I can say is, wow! It's no wonder lost people don't listen to what we say.
- I have a beautiful wife and seven really cool kids and I need to do a much better job of stewarding my time with them.
- When I see people like Joel Osteen, Paula White, Benny Hinn, Rod Parsley, and the staple 'preachers' on TBN, something inside me rises up in disgust. At first I occasionally watched for a bit of comic relief. I've since become sickened that these peddlers of heresy are pimping out such a perverted gospel to millions around the globe, and so many seem to be following them.
- The Spirit is willing, but my flesh is very, very weak.

# SUFFERING

I just left the hospital. No, I'm not sick. There's a student at the school where I teach who is in ICU. Long story short (and to protect his identity) let's say his name is Jack and he's in middle school. He is confined to a wheelchair. Nearly a week and a half ago, his wheelchair tipped over and he fell out. A trip to the ER confirmed nothing was broke and he was sent home. The following day, Jack was having difficulty breathing. Because of his condition (MD), he is already super susceptible to the sicknesses and viruses that most healthy bodies would fight off. Another trip to the ER revealed that Jack had pneumonia. So, for over a week now he's been in the pediatric ICU.

I just left there. What I saw broke my heart. He is hooked up to machines, cords, hoses, and cannot speak because he's on a respirator. He is incredibly uncomfortable, but cannot communicate what pains him because he has a tube down his throat to drain the excess fluids from his lungs caused from the pneumonia.

His mom and grandma were right there, one on each side of his bed. They didn't miss a beat. They knew when Jack was in pain but, as hard as they tried, there were times when there was simply not much they could do because it was so difficult to ascertain what was troubling him. The tube in his mouth made it virtually impossible for him to communicate.

Inside, I wept. I cannot even begin to imagine what it would be like to be the one caring for my own child like this. While standing in Jack's room, I imagined each one of my seven kids laying in his bed. That image was truly sobering. I am sometimes overwhelmed with this feeling that someday I will know the grief and despair that so many parents feel. I am certainly not a martyr, nor do I aspire to be one. However, the more God is revealing to me, the more I realize that only those who have walked the deep valleys of darkness and pain, can fully sympathize with others who are walking through their own dark and debilitating circumstances. And I desperately long for God to maximize my life on earth, so there are times when I find myself praying...."*Lord, do what You need to do so that the depth of my life and the scope of my ministry is maximized. I would selfishly choose to bypass the pain Lord, if that were an option. But, I know it's not. So, let it rain. Let it rain. I know that You are enough. You are sufficient.*"

I long to be a faithful minister of the gospel of Jesus Christ. Not just a preacher of John 3.16. I desperately want the beauty and majesty of the Sovereign Lord to be evident in what I teach, what I preach, how I live and how I love. And I'm becoming more and more convinced that this simply cannot happen to the fullest unless I am willing to join Paul in saying..."I want to know Christ and the power of His resurrection and the fellowship of sharing in His sufferings..." If I must suffer with You Jesus, teach me to suffer in a manner worthy of this high calling to....walk as You did.

Truth be told, my life is usually relatively pain free. Oh, don't get me wrong. We have our share of problems. Life is by no means a cake walk. But, our pain and suffering is miniscule compared to that of so many others.

I know the crippling pain caused from divorce. I understand the deep and lasting wounds inflicted from careless and unmeasured words. I am all too familiar with the pain of watching a mom struggle through life, just to make ends meet. I lost a brother five years ago to alcoholism. I remember the decision we made to turn off his life support machines. And I vividly remember holding his hand as he took his last breath. Those memories and images will no doubt affect me for the rest of my life. And today, my heart is so deeply grieved as I write and edit this book - my brother Darin just committed suicide. So, to some small degree, I understand pain and suffering. Sometime's my own, sometimes that of others.

My "suffering" doesn't even show up though on the scale of global suffering. Today, there are thousands of Christians around the globe who are locked in a dark prison, due to their unwavering allegiance to Jesus Christ. There are those alive today who have had their tongues cut out of their mouths because they would not recant their faith in God. Thousands, no doubt millions of Christ's followers have walked this road marked with genuine suffering, and breathed their last breath giving honor and glory to the Lord Jesus. I've read accounts of followers of Jesus who were unwavering in declaring their love for and trust in the sovereign Lord as they were being burned alive. I've known parents who have had to bury their child. I worked with a woman who ran over her own daughter. Days later I attended the funeral and watched this dear mother weep. I've been face to face with friends in Africa who have lost loved ones to AIDS. I've spent time with young men who had to

149

move dead bodies out of polluted, bloody puddles in order to find water during years of civil war in Liberia. I've walked alongside of parents who have spent their entire lives caring for their mentally and physically handicapped children. I've wept over my own siblings who have not been able to embrace the glory of the gospel and who continue to be plagued by the pain of our past and the consequences of destructive, life altering decisions they've made in an attempt to escape the hardships of life.

My "suffering" is not worth comparing though. It doesn't compare. The genuine suffering of others makes my "suffering" look like child's play. And by all accounts it *is* child's play.

Indeed, Paul must have had a myriad of his own bazaar thoughts about suffering when he uttered words like....

- *"For it has been granted to you that for the sake of Christ you should not only believe in Him but also suffer for His sake..."* **Philippians 1.29**
- *"I count everything a loss because of the surpassing worth of knowing Christ Jesus my Lord. For His sake I have suffered the loss of all things and count them as rubbish..."* **Philippians 3.8**
- *"...that I may know Him and the power of His resurrection, and may share in His sufferings..."* **Philippians 3.10**

- *"For I consider that the sufferings of this present time are not worth comparing with the glory that is to be revealed to us."* **Romans 8.18**

What is it that is so glorious that even the depths of pain and suffering cannot compare? What Treasure did Paul find that enabled him to say, *"...Christ will be honored in my body, whether by life or by death. For to me, to live is Christ and to die is gain."*?[3]

I think it was this – the unwavering belief that there is a sovereign God who is currently seated on His throne in heaven, and who is working to the ends that all the nations will one day, in the not so distant future, see His immense worthship clearly, fall before Him in utter humility, and declare with their lips that Jesus Christ is Lord, to the glory of God the Father.

That day is coming. And for those of us who are believers, we can take great courage in holding out for that day. And today, we can rest knowing that...our present sufferings are not worth comparing to the greatness of knowing Christ Jesus our Lord. *"Lord Jesus, make the cry of our hearts be this – that the Lamb receive the full reward of His suffering, in our living, in our dying, and in our suffering."*

# WHEN WILL IT BE MORNING?

Not sure how this will work. I feel like I'm totally consumed with the difficult and numbing process of grieving, and yet I know if I wait until it all makes sense, I may never write again. Here is my attempt to put some words to the horror of my life.

I am the youngest of six children. I grew up in a highly dysfunctional family. Both of my parents were alcoholics. God graciously saved my mom when she was pregnant with me. Unfortunately though, my mom and dad divorced when I was seven. As I grew up, I saw my dad for a few weeks out of the summer. By all accounts though, the relationship between us has always been skewed at best. My earliest memories consist of my dad cussing at me while telling me how worthless, incompetent, flawed and pathetic I was. I have few positive memories as they relate to my younger years with my father. As much as it pains me to write those words, they are true.

My five older siblings and I all grew up with our own twisted self image and deteriorated sense of value. From our earliest days, we each had a common heart condition – it was that we believed that we somehow did not belong, were completely inept and therefore were not worthy to exist. An accurate assessment would be that we each found different ways to attempt to anesthetize this enormous pain and heartache that we lived with each day of our lives.

As I mentioned, I am the youngest of six kids. I am forty and my oldest brother is fifty three. Each of us were affected by our home life differently and we've each responded to it and compensated for it in different ways. But, if you spend any significant amount of time with my family you'd quickly see where the fractures are and the affects of growing up in this kind of destructive environment.

Unfortunately though, the affects were more obvious and more devastating for two of my brothers. For one of my brothers, Dwight, I cannot count on one hand how many times I remember seeing him sober over the past twenty years. He was by all accounts a functioning alcoholic. His life was ruled by his desire and consumption of alcohol. Our family gatherings were all greatly affected by his presence because he was always acting under the influence of whatever liquor he had consumed that day. It was heartbreaking to watch him waste so much of his life trying to drink away his pain.

Darin was the brother I was closest to and is five years my senior. I've spent more time with him than probably all of my other siblings combined. Because we were closer in age, our lives intersected more as we were growing up and thankfully our bond continued through adulthood. When my parents divorced, my mom moved away with me, Darin, and my only sister Denise.

From the time I was about 8 or 9, I remember Darin going out and coming home smelling funny. I didn't know what pot smelled like back then. His recreational pot use later turned into a recreational use of alcohol and cocaine. Into his adult life, his frequent use of drugs and alcohol seemed to invade and disable his desire to live a normal, healthy, functional life. Darin would have days, weeks, sometimes even months where he would live without the influence of drugs. But, early on a pattern developed. He seemed to be caught in a vicious cycle somewhere between (clean and functioning) and (abusing and emotionally/physically MIA). This too was incredibly painful to watch. Countless efforts to help and intervene by many of those involved in Darin's life would bear only temporal results. It wouldn't be long before the destructive and devastating cycle of abuse would repeat itself, each time yielding greater consequences and deeper pain and turmoil to Darin and those closest to him.

Five years ago my brother Dwight killed himself by an overconsumption of liquor. For several years the doctors told him that if he didn't stop drinking it would end his life. One year before his death, his doctor reiterated this critical warning and told Dwight that if he didn't stop drinking he would be dead within a year.

I'll never forget the phone call. I was working outside in our yard with some college students. My brother Darin called and told me that Dwight was bleeding internally and that he was being rushed by ambulance to the hospital. I ran to the airport and hopped on the next flight to Ohio. I arrived that evening only to find that my brother was already on life support.

For two long weeks we watched as the machines did for him what his body was unable to do for itself. From time to time, he would respond to verbal commands to squeeze our hands. Throughout the two week 24/7 vigil we kept in Dwight's ICU room, there were several times that the doctors told us that his internal bleeding had started again and they would need to perform surgery to tie off the bleeding. This happened three or four times during the two weeks Dwight spent on life support.

One evening we left for dinner, which was a rarity because we really never left his room. This evening, we left to head home to clean up and grab dinner. Our plans were quickly altered by a phone call from the hospital telling us that we needed to make our way back immediately. Without question, we knew we were getting ready to walk through an unforgettable evening.

When we arrived, the doctors told us that Dwight had more internal bleeding and that they would not be able to do anything to stop it. We were left with two choices - we could let him bleed to death which the doctors told us would probably take about 24 hours. Or we could turn off his life support machines and end his life immediately.

After a short, emotionally charged family conference, we decided to turn off the machines that were keeping my brother alive. We did our best to process the events that were unfolding around us, said our good-bye's and stood by his bed and held his hands as the machines were turned off and his body stopped breathing. Four days later I performed Dwight's funeral and later that day we buried his body.

Those were three of the most difficult weeks I've ever lived through. I cannot even begin to tell you what it was like. If you've lived through something similar, you understand. If you haven't, then you probably don't and perhaps can't understand the depth of pain and sadness one feels. I remember coming back to my home in North Carolina and having what amounted to be a physical, emotional and spiritual meltdown. I just found the pain and sadness consumed the entirety of my life. That lasted for several months before God eventually lifted the consuming darkness that had enveloped me.

Fast forward five years. In late November 2010 I got a phone call that my brother Darin was missing and he had gotten his hands on several thousand dollars. So, after twenty four hours and lots of detective work it was discovered that my brother had had contact with a local drug dealer and was more than likely alive, but had consumed an incredibly large amount of crack cocaine.

As I was making my flight preparations to get to Ohio, I got the call that Darin had been found. He somehow ended up at a local hospital and they were currently holding him in the emergency mental health wing for assessment. The story of what unfolded during the following week is long, convoluted and incredibly painful. One I plan on sharing someday, but not now.

For now, you should know that after many years of watching my brother weave his way through the destructive cycle of his addictions and mental illness, most of my family agreed that after this last episode the only thing we could do for my brother to help him was to encourage him and assist him in getting in-patient and long term therapy in some kind of treatment facility.

The short version of the story is, our efforts of planning and pleading failed. My brother decided that he didn't need the treatment and was going to make another attempt at getting his life together, making better decisions, keeping his medications regulated, attending AA meetings, etc, etc, all without the help of any outside agency or medical supervisor. He was in essence going to make this work on his own, a futile effort he had made countless times in years past.

On January 25th at 11.30 in the morning I received a call that will be etched into my memory for the rest of my life. My oldest brother's wife was calling from my mom's phone. When I answered it, I was expecting to hear my mom's voice. Instead, my sister-in-law said "Dirk, it's Sue. Darin hung himself."

I cannot even begin to tell you how instantaneously dark things got. I fell to the floor and wept for what seemed like an eternity. I could not escape the haunting images in my mind of my brother hanging himself and I was unable to process the incredible depth of sadness that my heart was feeling. All I could do was weep and wail.

It hasn't even been three weeks yet. Some days I feel like it happened yesterday, other days I feel like I've been walking through this hellish pain for years. And perhaps in some ways I have. I don't know.

What I do know is this – God has been preparing me for this season of pain, sadness and suffering. I don't feel ready for it, but I'm confident that God has been working on my heart to equip me to process it and respond to it in ways that will ultimately make much of His sufficiency and greatness. Today though, I'm just trying to make it through the day without a meltdown, which is proving to be far more difficult than I care to admit.

I must say, I love my family deeply. Each of my brothers and my sister are incredible people. Dwight and Darin were two extraordinary human beings. Of course, like all of us, they each had their own junk to manage and navigate through. But, aside from all of that, they were amazing people. Huge hearts, creative, talented, generous, gregarious, great golfers, one was an introvert while the other was an extrovert, but both were the life of the party. If you walked into a room, you'd just need to listen for the most noise. Wherever the most noise was, there you would find both of my brothers. People around them were laughing and enjoying a moment that would no doubt be etched into their minds for years to come. That's just the type of people my brothers were.

But, they're gone now. There are no more parties. There is no more laughter. The noise has all been eclipsed by the deafening sounds of sadness and grief. This road marked with suffering is indeed a painful one, but one I know must be walked in order for there to be a triumphant display of the magnitude of the grace and glory of God.

For months now, I've been praying that God would allow me to experience a degree of suffering that would deepen my understanding of His sovereignty and also better equip me for the ministry He has called me to. And here I am. I suppose at the time I really didn't know the gravity of what I was asking for.

Some days I can't quite figure out how to get my clothes on the right way. Other days I don't even have the desire to breath. My heart aches. It hurts. Not just emotionally but it actually hurts physically. I've cried more than I thought was possible. I fall asleep thinking about my brothers and wake up thinking about them. Most of my days are consumed with thoughts of the final hours of Darin's life. It's hard to escape those haunting images as I learn to process this grief and sadness.

I have great friends who I know are praying for me. They've delivered food, sent cards, emails, texts, left messages, visited, etc. I also have an amazing wife and seven really sweet children who are also very sad. In their own ways of course. It seems it's been significantly less debilitating and easier for them to "move on" than it is for me. I don't know exactly what "moving on" looks like, but it doesn't feel as if it's on the immediate horizon for me.

So, why am I blogging about this? Truthfully, I'm not sure. Most days of late I feel like I don't have anything of value to share with anyone. My heart seems awfully achy and incapable of doing much for others at the moment. Some day, I believe this story will be told and it will be clear. And I believe that God will use it to make much of His name and renown. I also believe He will use it to minister to others, either those walking through their own misery or those living with the aftermath of the tragedy of suicide and loss.

But, today is today. I honestly don't really feel like I have much to offer. I selfishly hope that what I'm writing will prove to be therapeutic for me. I also hope the pain and chaos of my life can somehow help you find hope and healing with what you might be walking through yourself.

From the first moments that I could put words to my pain, I was saying…'God, I am very weak. But You are strong and Your power is made perfect in my weakness. Your grace is sufficient for today and Your mercies are new every morning.' That really is the extent of what I could get out of my mouth.

There are few things that ease the pain today, but the Scriptures that God has been leading me to are these:

- **Psalm 119.27** *'My soul melts away for sorrow; strengthen me according to Your Word.'*
- **Psalm 119.50** *'This is my comfort in my affliction, that Your promise gives me life.'*
- **Psalm 119.68** *'You are good and what You do is good.'*
- **Psalm 56.3** *'When I am afraid, I will put my trust in You.'*
- **Psalm 56.8** *'You have kept count of my tossing's, put my tears in Your bottle.'*
- **Psalm 56.12-13** *'I must perform my vows to You, O God; I will render thank offerings to You. For You have delivered my soul from death, yes my feet from falling, that I may walk before God in the light of life.'*
- **Psalm 91.15** *'When he calls to Me, I will answer him; I will be with him in trouble, I will rescue him and honor him.'*

I usually fall asleep listening to Steven Curtis Chapman's CD Beauty Will Rise. I resonate with Steven's heart when he sings:

"I don't even want to breathe right now, all I wanna do is close my eyes, but I don't wanna open them again, until I'm standing on the other side. I don't even wanna be right now, I don't wanna think another thought, and I don't wanna feel this pain I feel, but right now pain is all I've got. It feels like it's all I've got, but I know it's not, and I know You're all I've got...and I will trust You, I'll trust You, trust You God I will, even when I don't understand, even then I will say again, You are my God and I will trust You."

The previous pages are just a small glimpse into a few of my journal and blog entries. Why share these, you might be asking? Well, because my hope is that they paint a picture of a heart that desperately wants to follow Jesus and make much of His name and renown. My desire is that what I've written would give you a snapshot of what it looks like when God takes a heart and transforms it so that over time it looks more and more like the heart of Jesus. My writings obviously don't reveal someone who has it all together or has it all figured out. Quite the opposite really. The entries I've included here reveal a heart that is wickedly dark at its very core, yet longs to be so in love with Jesus that every fiber of my being screams *"Jesus You are worthy and I love You!"*

If we're going to get serious about the call God has on our lives, individually and corporately, we must reject the false notion that radical discipleship is reserved for the professionals or those who've signed up for level two of Christianity. There are no professional Christians and the idea of a two level

Christianity is nothing short of a perverted and dangerous heresy.

God is calling each of us to abandon our lives for the sake of the gospel. Jesus was clear two thousand years ago and is equally clear today - following Him is indeed an all or nothing proposition. He unapologetically and unequivocally demands our all.

Do you remember Stephen and Paul? The vivid New Testament accounts of their stonings should not be seen as anomalies in our spiritual assessment of what a radical follower of Jesus looks like. The way they lived and the way they died are indeed hallmarks of many professing disciples of Jesus. Both then and now.

This then begs the question, what happens if we give Him our all? What is God's blueprint for using a remnant of radical followers of Jesus to reach the nations of the world and gather together worshippers from every tribe and tongue and nation and people? Is it even possible that God would take a few ordinary people like you and me and start a movement that could quite possibly impact the entire globe? Let's explore that in the next chapter. But first, let's pray together.

## OUR PRAYER

*Before the mountains were made and even before You formed the earth and the world, from everlasting to everlasting You are God. You are the Mighty One, God the Lord who speaks and summons the earth from the rising of the sun to the place where it sets.*

*Lord, You are my light and my salvation; whom shall I fear? You are the stronghold of my life; of whom shall I be afraid?*

*Make me to know Your ways, O Lord. Teach me Your paths. Lead me in Your truth and teach me, for You are the God of my salvation.*

*I will tell of Your name to my brothers. In the midst of the congregation I will praise You. All the ends of the earth shall remember and turn to You, Lord. All the families of the nations shall worship before You. For kingship belongs to You, Lord, and You rule over the nations.*

*I will run in the way of Your commandments when You enlarge my heart. Please let the words of my mouth and the meditations of my heart be pleasing in Your sight O Lord, my Rock and my Redeemer. Keep me from presumptuous and willful sins so that they don't rule over me.*

*Satisfy me today with Yourself that You might be glorified in my life. Amen.*

# 7

# THE MULTIPLICATION BLUEPRINT

## JUST DO THE MATH

Over the past 20 years I've seen a number of different church growth plans, most of which, humanly speaking, are quite impressive. We cast our visions before our congregations and youth groups, trusting that our people will latch on to them, take ownership for them, and then help us fulfill those visions.

I'm not suggesting that there is anything wrong with casting a clear, God-honoring, Christ-exalting, Biblically sound vision for our people to embrace. After all, Jesus Himself cast a vision for His own life and ministry. And He did it in such a way as to give the general public a chance to embrace it and to build their lives around it. Jesus also gave a select few individuals an inside look at specific components of His vision that most others were not privy to.

So I'm all for casting the vision. Here's where I tend to get hung up though. It appears that many churches around the country have developed their own tailor-made church growth plans and strategies that have little or no connection to God's master plan to reach and teach the world, as He's revealed it in Scripture.

North American churches spend hundreds of millions of dollars each year hiring teams and companies to come in and tell them how to reach more people and grow larger churches. The problem with that is, among other things, it places the primary focus on our man-made efforts and strategies. It also distracts our focus from the sovereignty of God and the wooing of the Spirit of God in a person's life. All things considered, it seems rather antithetical to the approach and pattern we find in the New Testament.

The Biblical model of evangelism found in **Romans 10** goes something like this: God sends His servants. His servants preach and teach. People hear. Some who hear believe. Those who believe call. Everyone who calls is saved. Those who are saved get sent. And the process continues to repeat itself until the whole world has heard and Jesus returns.

Now, couple that model of evangelism with the model of making disciples laid out in **Matthew 28**, and we find God's master plan for reaching the globe with the gospel and making disciples of all the nations.[1] Clearly we are *all* called to take part in this plan. It is not reserved for the spiritually elite. God did not devise this strategy for full-time pastors and overseas missionaries. Lest you think you're off the hook, you're not. The plans laid out in Romans 10 and Matthew 28 have our names written all over them. Together, we have been appointed and called to be ambassadors of Jesus Christ, taking His message of reconciliation to a lost and broken world and making disciples of all the nations.

Some readers may look at these two different passages and claim they are more descriptive, rather than prescriptive. Descriptive would imply they are in our Bibles to simply relay information, giving specific details and mandates predominantly for a particular group of people at a particular time in history, with little or no implications for us.

Prescriptive would be more like a command or a directive given with the assumption that all who were privy to the information would respond to what they heard. In other words, if these passages were prescriptive rather than descriptive, they would have direct and radical implications for all of us who claim to be followers of Christ.

I believe it's clear that the two passages we're talking about are indeed prescriptive, not just descriptive. God was in fact giving us clear mandates to follow, both then and now. And with God's master plan so clearly laid out in Scripture, it's still baffling to see the astronomical amount of time and resources people waste trying to reinvent the wheel.

Our elaborate plans and blueprints to bring in the masses might just do that, bring in the masses. But our job is not to entertain the crowds or grow large churches. Our job is to vigilantly preach and teach until the whole world has been reached. Anything short of a model taken from Romans 10 and Matthew 28 to take the gospel to the world and make disciples of all the nations, will fall painfully short of the explicit mandates we've clearly been given in these two passages.

It's obvious that many of our man-made strategies do in fact produce visible results. Our numbers may increase, our giving may increase, the percentage of those participating in our programs and ministries might also increase. And if the standard by which we were called to evaluate our effectiveness had anything to do with numbers, these results would be impressive and quite encouraging to look at. But, we must keep in mind God's standard for evaluating our obedience is not our ingenuity or our creativity or the volume of warm bodies we can get to participate on a given Sunday. I would even suggest that God's standard of evaluating our obedience doesn't even have anything to do with the number of converts or baptisms we register each year. Our lives and ministries will ultimately be measured by our adherence to His revealed Word. God is solely responsible for whatever growth takes place.

As painful as it is to hear this, if the focus and thrust of our programs and ministries do not ultimately line up with the mandate and model He's given us in Romans 10 and Matthew 28, we've failed. I realize that may seem rather harsh. And perhaps it would be harsh if it were not true. However, the truth is sobering and we must all take heed to it. I'd much rather someone tell me now that what I'm doing doesn't properly line up with the Word of God, while I still have time to make some course corrections. The stark reality is, there will come a day in the not too distant future when it will be too late to make these changes.

It would behoove us all then to be intentional and specific when it comes to following God's plan as it is revealed in Scripture. We must take the gospel to the four corners of the earth and make Biblical disciples of all the nations. Every single one of the ministries in our churches need to ultimately fall under these two categories. We need to be actively taking the gospel to those who need to hear it and equipping those in our flocks to do the same. In addition to that we need to be actively and intentionally making disciples as outlined in Matthew 28.

Before we get to the specifics of how we accomplish all of this, let's look at the two most popular models that are being used today around the world. Let's call the first model, Strategy M (M for masses). Let's call the second model, Strategy D (D for discipleship).

Strategy M is employed by churches all over the globe. The basic goal of strategy M is to get as many people as possible assimilated into our programs and ministries. I was looking at a website yesterday of a prominent African American Pastor who preaches to his Georgia congregation of 20,000 on Sunday's and he preaches to an arena full of his other congregants in New York on Saturday's. His goal is obviously to preach to the masses. His strategy is not unlike the strategy of tens of thousands of pastors around the globe. We desire to fill coliseums and stadiums, church buildings and gymnasiums with throngs of people, so they can hear the Word of God preached. And maybe that's not all bad. But certainly we'd have to acknowledge that if we continue preaching to the same crowd without intentionally calling them to and equipping them for authentic, radical, Biblical discipleship, we've failed. Plain and simple. We can package it up and make it sound much more impressive and attractive. But, our non-discipleship Christianity will continue to be Christianity without Christ, which is really no Christianity at all. At some point we must recognize there exists a giant breakdown and disconnect with Strategy M.

People come, they fill our buildings, we preach our messages, they leave and come back next week for more. And because our buildings are full and there are no vacant chairs in sight, we make the assumption that we must be doing it right and God is obviously blessing our work. And perhaps in some cases He is.

But we should not equate numbers with blessing. We must not mistake a full building with anointing. It would be dangerous and erroneous for us to equate faithful attendance to Biblical discipleship.

Scripture clearly teaches that the time will come when people will not put up with sound doctrine. Instead, to suit their own desires, they will gather around them a great number of teachers to say what their itching ears want to hear. They will surround themselves with those unwilling to take a hard stand against American Christianity that boasts shallow and benign feel-good theology.[2] It is obvious even to a casual observer, that time has come. Many folks are just looking for someone who will tell them what they want to hear, stroke their egos, and tend to their felt needs. And pastors whose aim it is to do this don't have to work hard to fill their buildings on a given Sunday morning. Throngs of people flock to this type of message where the benefits are maximized and the costs are virtually eliminated.

When our message is that God loves you, has a wonderful plan to bless your life, (which includes but is not limited to a nicer car, a bigger home, a more secure savings account, a healthy life and a host of angels assigned to us to protect our assets), it's not hard to see why the stadiums fill up so fast. And why people will actually pay money to hear this junk. Of course, that might seem extreme to some of us. Unfortunately though, it's quickly becoming the accepted norm.

The fact is, we mistake preaching with disciple making. And clearly, they are not one in the same. We must acknowledge the fact that if we don't have intentional disciple making strategies connected directly to our proclamation of the Word, we've failed. We cannot preach the message of the cross week after week without consistently giving a clear explanation of what it costs to be a disciple and make other disciples.

Our preaching and teaching must be coupled with a comprehensive strategy that people can both understand and get involved with. This demands we articulate a clear strategy that walks people through the process of becoming a radical disciple and thoroughly equips them to reproduce themselves by making other radical disciples.

Over the past two days, I've spent time with two different youth pastors from two different parts of the country. Each of these guys have very different philosophies of ministry, which no doubt stem from very different theologies and different understandings of the core of the gospel.

Barry is from the Midwest. He has an average size youth group ranging from 40-60, depending on the week. Zack is from the West Coast. He too has an average size youth group that fluctuates a bit, depending on school calendars and extracurricular activities that week. Both have about 10-12 adult youth workers ministering alongside of them.

Barry's been at this church for almost two years. When he first arrived, much of the time on Sunday's and Wednesday's was devoted to games and group activities. Barry has been intentional about doing away with the games in an effort to spend as much time as possible teaching his students the Word of God. His goal is to invest his time in making disciples. He is equipping his youth workers to do the same, with the goal that each student will leave his youth ministry one day and go on to zealously make other disciples.

Zack has been at his church for about two and a half years now. Zack's approach is much different than Barry's. He spends a large part of his youth budget on outreach events designed to provide a certain level of entertainment and fun for his students, while giving them a place to invite their lost friends.

Both of these approaches are being employed by youth pastors from all over the world. Unfortunately, it seems that Zack's methodologies are far more popular and are being used by more youth pastors than Barry's approach.

As Barry and I sat together and talked about the value in what he's doing, I encouraged him to stay the course. Even when it seems numbers are going backwards (and sometimes they will), stay the course. Even when parents are moaning and groaning (and sometimes they will) because you're not playing cool games like the old youth pastor used to do, stay the course. And even when no one else seems to get what you're doing (and sometimes they won't), just stay the course.

It's not often I see youth pastors cry, but God has given Barry a very tender heart for his students. He knows many of them are missing the boat. He understands the pressure his students are facing to conform to the world. He longs to see them embrace a purpose for living that transcends culture, denominations, age, and ethnicities. He desires that his students would fall madly in love with Jesus so that they will gladly waste their lives making much of His name among the nations. Talking about all this causes tears to well up in his eyes and stream down his face. I'm grateful for guys like Barry whose deep love for God manifests itself in a genuine love and brokenness for the spiritual condition of other people.

As we sat and talked, we discussed the following scenario. Suppose I can fill a stadium each night with 15,000 people. I don't mean just on Sunday's either. I mean, let's say for 30 days straight I can fill a stadium with 15,000 people and each night share the gospel with those people. At the end of the month, I've preached to an impressive cumulative crowd of 450,000.

Now, enlarge the plan. Let's say I preach to a crowd of 15,000 people every night for an entire year. Do the math. The numbers are quite impressive. No less than 5,475,000 people over the course of twelve months will hear the message. That's an enormous amount of people.

Let's say I do this same thing every night of the year for a period of thirty years. This would total 164,250,000 people. No doubt those numbers are staggering and this is indeed an astronomical amount of people we're talking about.

Of course we don't live in a vacuum so this hypothetical model is a bit flawed. If a believer comes one night and they bring four of their unbelieving friends, do they count as four or five? If ten people from my church attend and only bring one lost person, do they count as eleven or one? You see where I'm going with this? Not all of the 15,000 in attendance are truly unregenerate people who are hearing the gospel for the first time. So, that affects our numbers to a large degree.

Couple that with the fact that if you're a Christian who has lost friends and neighbors, do you really need to drag them to an 'event' where someone else preaches the gospel? Is this really the best approach to sharing with them the radical message of Jesus? Doesn't it diminish the message and undermine the power of transformation if we walk away from our role as ambassadors in delivering this message of reconciliation and relegate it to the "professionals"?

Does God really intend for us to delegate this sharing of the gospel to other people? Don't we have a responsibility ourselves to carry the gospel to our neighbors and friends? Why have we become comfortable abdicating our responsibility and relegating this mandate to others?

It is indeed our job to share the gospel with the world and make disciples of the nations. Our job. Not their job, or his job, or her job. It's our job. We have been called and assigned this kingdom task. Passing this responsibility off to the "professionals" or to someone else is simply not a Biblical option and it is tantamount to flagrant disobedience.

In 2 Corinthians 5.17-20, we can clearly see that God has indeed called those of us who have been redeemed, to be His ambassadors who take the message of reconciliation to the rest of the world.

> "Therefore, if anyone is in Christ, he is a new creation. The old has passed away; behold, the new has come. All this is from God, who through Christ reconciled us to Himself and *gave us the ministry of reconciliation*; that is, in Christ God was reconciling the world to Himself, not counting their trespasses against them, and *entrusting to us the message of reconciliation*. Therefore, *we are ambassadors for Christ*, God making His appeal through us."

We find a very similar message in 1 Peter 2.9-10. This passage is packed full of deep truths that have significant implications of our redemption and the very purpose for our existence. Peter makes it absolutely clear that we have been redeemed so that we will be a beacon for the grace and mercy that can be found in the redemptive work of Jesus Christ.

The descriptive words Peter uses for and about believers is not just to make us feel good. Rather to make clear to us the responsibility and obligation that comes along with being a redeemed follower of Jesus Christ.

> "You are a chosen race, a royal priesthood, a holy nation, a people for His own possession, that you may *proclaim* the *excellencies* of Him who called you out of darkness into His marvelous light. Once you were not a people, but now you are God's people; once you had not received mercy, but now you have received mercy."

Notice the words *proclaim* and *excellencies*. Proclaim means to herald; to publish; to advertise; to tell of something otherwise unknown. The word excellencies implies the ability to perform powerful and heroic deeds and not just the miracles Jesus performed during His ministry either. This word refers primarily to the extraordinary work of redemption.

You can see that Peter holds no punches when he says that it is *our* responsibility as followers of Jesus Christ to declare to those who are lost in the world that Jesus has made a way for them to be redeemed and reconciled to God. The responsibility belongs to us. Not our pastors and not the evangelists. Us.

In any case, as impressive as the net results are for Strategy M (remember upwards of 164 million people), let's take a look at the strategy Jesus employed and the one I encouraged my friend Barry to embrace. We're calling it Strategy D.

In Strategy D, we start with two discipler's each discipling one person for a period of two years. At the end of two years our numbers are less than impressive. We've made a whopping total of two disciples. If both of these new disciples find two other people to disciple themselves, and assuming the original two discipler's continue to disciple others, at the end of four years we're made a meager six disciples. Still nothing to write home about. And quite frankly, it's very difficult to see how this strategy would be more effective than Strategy M.

If you look at the chart on the following pages and follow the same pattern we followed for the first four years, you'll begin to see the dramatic affects of multiplication. You'll discover that starting with two discipler's who both disciple one person each theoretically yields over nine million disciples in thirty years. Granted, that's only if each person is faithful to invest in making disciples of others.

Still not impressed? Still not convinced this strategy is the best one? Of course not, because in Strategy M we preached to more than 164 million people in just thirty years. With Strategy D we've only made disciples of nine million people during those same thirty years. A far cry from the figures Strategy M boasts.

Big difference though. With Strategy M we are simply preaching to the masses. In Strategy D we are actively and intentionally making disciples. Polar opposite strategies and equally as diverse results. Strategy M boasts quantity and width. Strategy D strives for quality and depth.

Keep analyzing Strategy D. If you follow Strategy D for ten more years, you'll see we've theoretically made disciples of over two billion people.

Now add two more years. Starting with our original two discipler's and two disciplee's, after forty two years of investing in the strategy of Jesus we've theoretically made disciples of nearly seven billion people. And just two short years later, forty four years after we initiated this strategy, we've made disciples of nearly twenty one billion people, three times the earth's current population.

After ten years, with two initial discipler's making disciples who continue to reproduce themselves, we've made a total of 162 disciples. If we increase the number of initial discipler's to four, you can see from the chart below that it expedites the process exponentially.

Check out the results after ten years if we double our initial investment. Instead of ending up with 162 disciples after ten years we end up with two thousand five hundred disciples after those same ten years. It truly is mind boggling how the Biblical process of reproducing disciples can reach such a staggering number of people in what amounts to be such a relatively short amount of time.

The chart below records the multiplying results attained with Strategy D

| A | B | C | D |
|---|---|---|---|
| 2 | 2 | 3 | 4 |
| 4 | 6 | 12 | 20 |
| 6 | 18 | 48 | 100 |
| 8 | 54 | 192 | 500 |
| 10 | 162 | 768 | 2,500 |
| 12 | 486 | 3,072 | 12,500 |
| 14 | 1,458 | 12,288 | 62,500 |

| 16 | 4,374 | 49,152 | 312,500 |
|----|-------|--------|---------|
| 18 | 13,122 | 196,608 | 1,562,500 |
| 20 | 39,366 | 786,432 | 7,812,500 |
| 22 | 118,098 | 3,145,728 | 39,062,500 |
| 24 | 354,294 | 12,582,912 | 195,312,500 |
| 26 | 1,062,882 | 50,331,648 | 976,562,500 |
| 28 | 3,188,646 | 201,326,592 | 4,882,812,500 |
| 30 | 9,565,938 | 805,306,368 | 24,414,062,500 |
| 32 | 28,697,814 | 3,221,225,472 | 122,070,312,500 |
| 34 | 86,093,442 | 12,884,901,888 | 610,351,562,500 |
| 36 | 258,280,326 | 51,539,607,552 | 3,051,757,812,500 |
| 38 | 774,840,978 | 206,158,430,208 | 15,258,789,062,500 |
| 40 | 2,324,522,934 | 824,633,720,832 | 76,293,945,312,500 |
| 42 | 6,973,568,802 | 3,298,534,883,328 | 381,469,726,562,500 |
| 44 | 20,920,706,406 | 13,194,139,533,312 | 1,907,348,632,812,500 |

A: number of years
B: number of disciples produced starting with two disciples
C: number of disciples produced starting with three disciples
D: number of disciples produced starting with four disciples

Granted, there are only 7 billion people on the planet. An estimated 1 billion people are already active disciples of Jesus. And obviously not every person who participates in being a disciple will be faithful to make other disciples. It's a given that there will be a multitude of breakdowns along the way. It's assured that many of those who sign up to be a disciple and make other disciples will fall by the wayside. Look no further than Judas. And I can give you a list of those I've personally discipled who have wandered off. Certainly if you've spent any considerable time discipling people, you can testify to the same.

Looking at both strategies though and how effective they would both be given ideal circumstances, it's clear the strategy Jesus initiated and employed starting with His twelve disciples was an infinitely wise and ingenious strategy, not just to preach the gospel to the ends of the earth, but to also effectively make disciples of all the nations.

Strategy D isn't superior to Strategy M because it boasts larger numbers. It's simply the only viable model because it is the model and strategy Jesus employed. This strategy hinges on radical and passionate disciples committed to the process of making other radical and passionate disciples. And the heartbeat of this strategy is quality as opposed to quantity.

We're not simply preaching to the masses and then leaving them to fend for themselves in an effort to get as many people 'saved' as we possibly can. We're actively taking people, one at a time, and making them passionate followers of Jesus Christ. Not only does this produce deeper, Biblically literate, willful disciples of Jesus over the short term, but it multiplies our efforts over the long term. Strategy D clearly elevates a plan with a global impact capable of reaching the world with the gospel and making disciples of all the nations.

We should keep in mind, the goal is not simply conversions. Certainly, God wills that His elect respond to the message of the gospel by committing the totality of their lives to following hard after Jesus. And this process starts with conversion. But let's not lose sight of the fact that Jesus is looking for obedience to His commands. When Jesus said "go and make disciples, teaching them to obey all that I've commanded you," He chose the word *obey* because it was significant. He wasn't simply looking for some religious fanatics committed to following a strict code of moral conduct. He was calling for people who would love Him and His Father more than anything else.

Remember it was Jesus who said "If anyone loves Me, he will keep My word. Whoever does not love Me does not keep My words."[3]

At first glance Jesus' own strategy looks a bit pathetic and grossly inept. He chooses twelve very unlikely candidates and decides to use them to spread the message of His gospel. He doesn't pick the best, He certainly didn't pick the brightest, and He obviously didn't pick the most popular guys around. He handpicked an obscure and unknown group of guys, turned them into a renegade band of followers, and entrusted them with this radical message that would turn the world upside down.

Unbelievable. Simply unbelievable. Looking at this original model and how Jesus went about picking these men and how He invested in them seems ludicrous. It just doesn't appear that His strategy or approach was a good one. Looking at the original make-up of the group, including the dissention of Judas and the betrayal of Peter, makes us question whether this really is the best model to follow. Clearly though, it is not only the best model to follow, it is the model Jesus has called us and commanded us to adhere to and follow as well.

And what makes all this even more unbelievable is our blatant disregard for the revolutionary model Jesus initiated for us and our insatiable ambition to market a better strategy.

Clearly we have the most effective strategy on the globe at our disposal. The question is - will we commit the totality of our lives to carrying out Jesus' mission to preach the gospel to the world and make disciples of all the nations? Will we design our ministries and our programs to revolve around the strategy Jesus laid out for us, or will we continue wasting our resources trying to reinvent His master plan to preach the gospel to the world and make disciples of the nations?

At the heart of this issue, isn't it really just a matter of love and trust? Do we love God and His Word more than we love our own egos and agendas? Do we trust the Word of God to do what only the Word of God can do? Do we believe that God is faithful to Himself and faithful to accomplish His sovereign purposes? When we employ other strategies and try to figure out a better way to accomplish God's purposes, aren't we really saying, in essence, "God, I say I love You but my actions prove otherwise. I don't really trust You, and I don't believe that Your way is perfect."

Certainly none of us would say those words out loud, but when we disregard God's revealed plan and strategy, we are in essence saying that exact thing. This is clearly more of a heart issue than anything else. We need to be vigilant to ensure our hearts stay in tune with the heart of God. We must daily yield to His authority and wash our minds with His Word.

We cannot possibly expect our lives to bear kingdom fruit and bring honor to His name if we're attempting to blaze our own trail when it comes to rallying together worshippers from every tribe and language and people and nation whom Jesus has ransomed and whom God has purposed to redeem.

The trail has indeed been blazed. Jesus is leading this charge and unequivocally calling us to follow His lead. In doing so, our obedience will communicate our deep love for God and our trust in His sovereign and wise plan.

# OUR PRAYER

*It is true, Lord, that we have neglected Your strategy and taken up our own. We plan and forecast and often do so without Your consultation. Our flesh drives us and we are quick to overlook the revealed plans You've so graciously laid out for us in Scripture.*

*We confess our putrid sin before You. In an effort to boast about the ingenious strategies we employ, we neglect to consult You and we continually fail to embrace the clear and concise plan that You've revealed in Your Word.*

*You've given us the mandate to preach the gospel to the ends of the earth and to make disciples of all the nations. Instead of investing the totality of our lives fulfilling these mandates, we've squandered much of our wealth and our resources in an effort to grow bigger churches with bigger budgets, bigger programs, and bigger sanctuaries.*

*Your heart must be grieved. Would You continue to break our hearts for the very thing that breaks Your heart? Would You sensitize us to Your Spirit so we are never out of synch with what You are doing and what You are saying? We wander so quickly and stray so far. At times we just need to be corrected and brought back to the sheepfold. Thank You for being our Good Shepherd.*

*Your plan to reach and teach the world is going to work and we will gladly participate with You. All too often though we've failed to recognize that absolutely nothing of kingdom value will ever happen in us or through us as long as we attempt to blaze our own trails and follow our own ingenuity. We must simply find ourselves desperate for You as we purpose to live our lives with passion and purpose. The posture of our heart must be such that humility and simple obedience take the place of pride and independence.*

*We confess that Jesus Christ is Lord, to the glory of God the Father. This we pray for Jesus' sake. Amen.*

# DISCIPLE MAKING 101

## AREN'T ALL "CHRISTIANS" DISCIPLES

Suppose I was speaking at your church one Sunday morning. As I stood to deliver my message, I started by asking the congregation this simple question – "Is *this church* actively making disciples?" And I followed it up with another question – "Are *you* actively making disciples?" And then I concluded my questions by asking – "Does it matter how we go about making disciples?" What kind of responses do you think I would get?

As you can imagine the answers would vary according to the number and variety of people who summoned the courage to respond. There probably wouldn't be two answers alike. Some would agree that their church was actively making disciples. Others might say their church wasn't making disciples at all. Some would quickly contend that they were making disciples themselves, while others would argue they've never acquired the necessary skills for such a monumental and spiritual undertaking. Perhaps some would say it doesn't matter how we go about making disciples, just so long as we're making efforts. While others might protest and argue it does matter how we attempt to make disciples and we should ensure our strategies are intentional and we do it properly.

It would only make sense then that if indeed we are going to be faithful and obedient to the Word of God, and invest our time and resources in making disciples of the nations, we will need to have a clear, concise, Biblically aligned strategy to accomplish this monumental task. And this necessitates that we communicate this clearly with those around us so they are not in the dark about some of the following: what the end goal is; how the kingdom will be impacted; how God will be honored; how God's glory will be magnified; what is being required of them; and what it will ultimately cost them.

Any effective leader will tell you that casting a clear vision is necessary and having a detailed plan of execution is equally as vital. We cannot possibly hold people accountable, whether it be our kids, our accountability partners, folks in our congregation or Life Group, our students, etc, apart from having clear expectations and guidelines. It certainly would be far from fair to render someone liable if they've never been given the standard to which you are holding them accountable.

I'm grateful to the Lord that He doesn't just hold out some vague, random, illusive expectations and then demand that we meet His requirements. He certainly is not neutral in telling us how we should spend the remainder of our days on planet earth. Our mandate appears specific and clear from the pages of Scripture. Like I mentioned before, there most definitely are some gray areas in Scripture that leave room for debate and personal conviction. But when it comes to the mandate given in Matthew 28, we really don't have any wiggle room.

As we look at this passage, often referred to as the Great Commission in Matthew 28, it would be good for us to address a few preliminary questions before we dig in.

1. What is the primary task of the church?
2. How did Jesus spend the last three years of His life on planet earth?
3. What was the very last thing Jesus said before He ascended into heaven?

We can start with these three questions. Perhaps in answering these three questions we'll have a better understanding of the meaning and significance of the Great Commission in Mathew 28. So, let's tackle these one at a time.

### Question #1 – What is the primary task of the church?

In short, the number one objective of the church of Jesus Christ is to proclaim the gospel to the world and make disciples of the nations. It really comes down to these two specific assignments. The passages I'd refer you to are Matthew 28.16-20; Mark 16.15-16; and Luke 24.45-47.

### Matthew 28.16-20

*"Then the eleven disciples went to Galilee, to the mountain where Jesus had told them to go. When they saw Him, they worshipped Him; but*

185

*some doubted. Then Jesus came to them and said, 'All authority in heaven and earth has been given to Me. Therefore, go and make disciples of all nations, baptizing them in the name of the Father and of the Son and of the Holy Spirit, and teach them to obey everything I have commanded you. And surely I am with you always, to the very end of the age.'"*

**Mark 16.15-16**
*"And He said to them, 'Go into all the world and proclaim the gospel to the whole creation. Whoever believes and is baptized will be saved, but whoever does not believe will be condemned.'"*

**Luke 24.45-47**
*"Then He opened their minds so they could understand the Scriptures. He told them, 'This is what is written: The Messiah will suffer and rise from the dead on the third day, and repentance for the forgiveness of sins will be preached in His name to all nations, beginning at Jerusalem.'"*

It seems abundantly clear that Jesus has left us with the tasks of taking the gospel to every place on planet earth and making disciples of the people of all the nations. Simply put, that is the mission and mandate of the church, both then and now. We must not exchange His perfect design to make passionate followers of Jesus Christ with our paltry desires to grow bigger churches.

### Question #2 - How did Jesus spend the last three years of His life on this earth?

We know from Scripture that Jesus did a lot of different things while He roamed the streets of Jerusalem and the hillsides and shorelines of Galilee. He certainly kept busy doing His Father's work. It would be accurate to say Jesus spent the last three years of His time on earth performing miracles of many kinds, hanging out with lepers, criminals, social and religious outcasts, and taking a public stand against the stench of status quo religiosity which was void of the power and ability to redeem and transform.

There's an interesting passage in the beginning of Mark 10. Mark makes an important observation by saying *'As was His custom, He taught them.'* He taught them? Yep, He taught them. And this wasn't something unusual that Jesus reserved for the holy days. It was the custom and routine of Jesus to intentionally teach people truth, in any and every situation. Why did He do this? Why was there such emphasis placed on teaching them truth?

Because Jesus knew that truth was the key to lasting transformation. And Jesus wasn't looking for quick converts who would sign up for the latest religious fad. Jesus was seeking those who would worship in Spirit and Truth. He was looking for authentic, passionate followers who would be willing to lay down their own lives and take up their crosses to follow hard after Him.

A person's ability to hear and understand truth were foundational prerequisites for them in order to be able to apply that truth to their lives and experience the kind of lasting transformation that Jesus was offering. In order for a person to understand truth, they would first need to hear the truth and then God would need to reveal the essence of the truth in what they heard.

Does all this seem a bit complicated? It's really not. It's actually rather simple. Here's how the pattern of lasting transformation is typically seen throughout Scripture.

## REVELATION OF TRUTH
## + UNDERSTANDING OF TRUTH
## + APPLICATION OF TRUTH
## = TRANSFORMATION

I realize what I'm saying contradicts the teaching and experiences of many of my good friends who would describe themselves as charismatic or Pentecostal, or sometimes even a combination of the two. I even have some Baptist friends who tend to be a bit Pentecostal and like to refer to themselves as Bapticostal.

Much of the focus of charismatic teaching is on modern day miracles and the gifts of the Spirit. I would never disagree that God is indeed a miracle working God and is more than able to heal people's hearts, raise the dead, restore blind eyes, supernaturally feed the starving, etc, etc. I believe God can and does do miracles all the time. So I'm certainly not posturing that God no longer performs miracles or gives His gifts to believers.

My charismatic friends and I would tend to differ on several key aspects of important theology. For instance:

1.  I don't believe God's primary goal is to make everyone healthy.

2.  I certainly don't agree that a lack of deeper, more sincere faith is the primary cause of our physical ailments and spiritual diseases. If that were the case, how would you explain martyrs who suffer and die at the hands of those vehemently opposed to the gospel? Did they just not believe hard enough? And is a lack of faith seriously to blame for all of those who will starve to death today in Africa?

3.  God is far more interested in my sanctification than in me enjoying a comfortable life.

4.  To expect God to fix everything, without us walking through the process of identifying, confessing and repenting of our sins, seems to shortchange much of what we learn in the process of lasting transformation. The quick fixes also seem to unintentionally absolve us from taking personal responsibility for our lives.

5.  My charismatic friends tend to have an unbalanced focus on the more "spectacular" gifts of the Spirit,

with little or no emphasis on all of the other, less noticeable gifts that the Spirit gives us.

All of that just to say this – while there certainly are exceptions to the normal patterns we find in the Word of God, we can't focus solely on these exceptions. We must rather look at the normative pattern of God's activity as it's revealed throughout Scripture.

If the process of genuine, lasting, God-honoring, Christ-exalting transformation is going to take place in a person's life, there are several critical components that most often times are present in this process.

First, God must reveal something to this person. If we're going to read and understand anything at all in the Word of God, it'll only happen as the Spirit Himself reveals it to us. David said "Open my eyes, that I may behold wondrous things out of Your law."[1] We call this revelation.

Second, the person must understand what God revealed to them. Truth must be understood in general terms. If God reveals truth to us but we don't understand what He's saying, it cannot possibly bring about lasting transformation.

When Jesus was explaining the parable of the sower, He specifically referred to people who hear the words of the kingdom but do not understand what they are hearing. He said the evil one comes and snatches away what they hear before they are able to understand it.[2]

Once a person hears and understands truth, they must then make application of that revealed truth. Once a person does this, God wisely and graciously brings about His desired transformation. Again, when Jesus was explaining the parable of the sower, He said the person whose life produced fruit was the person who heard the Word AND understood what they heard.[3]

Simply hearing is not enough. If a person hears yet doesn't understand, the seed falls on infertile soil. Millions of people hear the truth of the gospel every day and yet remain unchanged. For instance, just because you hear someone speaking in another language does not mean you understand what they are saying. Most of us have overheard conversations in which people are speaking other languages and we have absolutely no idea what they are saying. We can hear them but we really have no clue what is being said. Audible sounds, no matter how loud they may be, do not transform depraved hearts.

Suppose a person hears and understands. Even this is not enough to bring about lasting transformation. There are scores of people who know and understand certain doctrinal truths and yet their lives are unchanged. No doubt the world is full of scholars who have heard the truth claims of Scripture and who understand what they mean. Yet, without internalizing that information and making personal application to it, ones heart remains unaffected.

Information and comprehension must be coupled with application. And looking at this process backwards we see that genuine application can't happen apart from understanding. Understanding can't happen apart from hearing. And hearing spiritual matters can only happen as the Spirit of God opens a person's mind and heart to that revelation.

According to Romans 12.2, our lives are transformed as our minds are renewed. Our minds are renewed only as old patterns of thinking are replaced with new information and a new way of thinking. We must have a changed outlook and altered perspective before there will be lasting transformation taking place in our lives.

So then, why was it the custom of Jesus to teach truth? Why do we find the heart of Jesus beating for people to understand clearly the heart of the Father? Simply because it was truth that paved the way for lasting transformation. The kind of transformation possible only by adhering to and obeying the voice of the One who calls Himself Master.

**Question #3 – What was the very last thing Jesus said before He ascended into heaven?**

For this we can look at the words recorded in Matthew 28.16-20. Jesus had already been resurrected and was making His appearances to many. He had seen Mary and Mary and had given them instructions to find the disciples and tell them to meet Him in Galilee.

Both Mary's quickly found the disciples and shared this astonishing news with them. The disciples then quickly made their way to Galilee to meet up with the resurrected Jesus. Mathew 28.17 records that when the disciples saw Him, they worshipped Him. Well, not all of them. Scripture records that some worshipped, while others doubted. In other words, some understood who He was and acknowledged His rightful place as Lord and Master. Others held back, not sure about worship and abandonment, about risking themselves totally.

Not much has changed in 2,000 years. Some see Jesus and gladly surrender all that they know about themselves to all that they know about Him. Others are more reluctant, not convinced Jesus is really worth the sum of their lives.

In any case though, when Jesus sees His disciples again He addresses them by reminding them of this very critical truth: all authority resides with Him. Jesus reiterated His rightful place as Lord and Master and Ruler of all. Before He lays out His strategy and how He plans on incorporating them into His global redemptive plan, He reminds them that He is indeed the One in charge. He alone stands as Supreme Authority over everything and everyone. He holds the power to call all the shots because the Father has indeed entrusted this authority to Him. So Jesus sets the stage by saying, "All authority in heaven and on earth has been given to Me."

In light of this authority, He is perfectly entitled and justified in mandating them (and us!) to "go and make disciples." They've now been handed the baton. Jesus has spent the previous three years investing in these men, teaching them, training them, equipping them, fashioning them into His likeness.

Jesus spent considerable time modeling Biblical discipleship for His disciples. Here's how it shook down: Initially, He worked and they watched. Then, He worked and called them to join Him in His Work. There came a point when Jesus turned the reigns over while He watched them work. At this point in the process of the change in leadership, they worked, and He was about to leave the scene. He had entrusted His disciples with the unbelievable objective of taking this life-changing truth and teaching it to others. Jesus was clear to stress the point that His emphasis was on properly equipping (teaching how to obey), not just transferring information.

This then begs the question – what exactly is a Biblical disciple? There are no doubt lots of disciples in the world. Buddhists have disciples. Muslims have disciples. Jehovah Witnesses have disciples. There are many different types of disciples with a variety of different goals. So what then was Jesus referring to when He called us to make disciples?

I can think of no greater works on this topic of Biblical discipleship then Bill Hulls book called *The Complete Book Of Discipleship* and Ray Vander Laan's workbook and video series called *In The Dust Of The Rabbi*. Both have been incredibly valuable to me over the years as I've studied Biblical discipleship and the intent of Jesus when He left us with this life consuming ambition to invest the totality of our lives making disciples of His. I highly recommend both of these works to you if you're serious about discovering all that it means to be both a radical disciple of Jesus and someone committed to the lifelong endeavor of making other disciples of Christ.

A disciple (Greek word *mathetes)* is a learner or follower, a student – usually someone committed to a significant master. Disciple is the primary term used in the gospels and Acts to refer to Jesus' followers. It was a common referent for those known in the early church as believers, Christians, brothers/sisters, those of the Way, or saints. In this sense, the term was used at least 230 times in the gospels and 28 times in the book of Acts.

In ancient Israel, rabbis had disciples who would commit a large portion of their lives to learning the Torah. They would sit at the feet of these rabbis, watching and listening to everything the rabbi said. It was the hope and desire of the disciple to one day be like the rabbi and be able to know the Torah and teach Scripture to others.

In essence discipleship is what a disciple does. If a professed "Christian" isn't following Christ, then Christ gets left out of the process and Biblical discipleship isn't taking place. And if Christ gets left out of this process, then one has just made an agreement with a set of facts, and isn't really committed to the task of Biblical discipleship. We must keep in mind though, that when someone claims to have faith in Christ, they must also commit to follow Christ.

Bill Hull notes: "The American gospel teaches that faith equals agreement with a set of religious facts. Believing in Jesus has no meaning if we don't follow Him in discipleship. Believing without discipleship isn't believing, it's agreeing to a set of facts about a religious figure. The problem we face is that we have created and taught a faith that doesn't transform people."[4] Saying we believe simply isn't enough. The demons believe, and shudder![5] Our faith must produce action. And genuine faith will produce action.

It's time we end this insanity and put a stop to perpetuating this heresy. We must be reminded and remind others that both Jesus and Paul taught that following Jesus is proof of being a Christian. The book of James affirms the same.

"The gospel of the kingdom Jesus delivered in the Sermon on the Mount is the same gospel preached in Acts and the same gospel Paul presented in Romans, Ephesians, Philippians, and Colossians. When Jesus commanded, "Make disciples," He wasn't simply referring to converts. He wants followers who follow – people who submit to His teachings and His ways."[6]

If we reexamine the Great Commission in Matthew 28, and look at the entirety of this passage, we find that Jesus told His disciples to make other disciples and teach them to obey. We must not overlook the thrust and aim Jesus had in mind when He delivered those words to these men.

He told them to teach people to obey. I've often asked people why they think Jesus used the word obey. Why didn't He tell them to make religious people? Or make church attenders? Or make moral people? Why did He tell them to teach people to obey? I think there is something significant here that often gets overlooked.

Jesus equated obedience with love. I'm not saying He equated morality with love, or good deeds with love. What Scripture teaches is that Jesus equates love with Biblical obedience.

If I willfully choose to obey Jesus, I am proving my love for Him. Should I choose to disobey Him, I am declaring by my actions that I don't love Him as I should. It's really as simple as that. Jesus and John said as much themselves. Jesus said, "If anyone loves Me, he *will* obey My teaching. Anyone who does *not* love Me will *not* obey My teaching." John said, "This is love for God, to obey His commands and His commands are not a burden."[7]

When we invest our lives rallying together a band of radical followers of Jesus, we are in essence growing the kingdom of God with people who will unashamedly join our anthem by proclaiming from the hilltops that we love Jesus! These aren't just benign words that roll off of our tongues. These words are an overflow of the posture of our hearts and are proven true by how we purpose to live our lives. In both word and deed we make much of His name among the nations. Remember, the first and most important commandment in both the Old and New Testaments was to love God more than anything and everything else. From the beginning of recorded Biblical history, God has made His desire and mandate clear — that He would be the object of our minds attention and our hearts affections. Clearly, love is a big deal to God.

It's true, making disciples can feel like a daunting task. We cannot escape the reality that it is a seriously costly endeavor and undertaking. As we learn to commit the whole of our lives to this, let's keep in mind Jesus' promise as He concluded the mandate He gave us in the Great Commission.

Jesus said, as you go to invest the whole of your lives by making disciples of the nations, keep in mind that you are not going alone. My presence will permeate your endeavors and your efforts will be maximized by My indwelling Spirit. Jesus assured us of this by saying, "I am with you always, to the end of the age."[8]

# OUR PRAYER

*I long to be a radical disciple of Yours, Jesus. You have indeed called me and commissioned me to represent You to the world. I've been entrusted with a radical message of reconciliation and You've made it clear that You are looking for those who will gladly forsake their own lives in an effort to pick up their cross and follow You. Help me to be that kind of person. The truth is, I fail more than I succeed. I'm often more cowardly than courageous. I am marked by selfishness rather than selflessness. My heart rarely beats the way You redeemed it to beat. I am still very much tainted by the depth of my own sin.*

*You can free me from my self-centered life and empower me to exhaust my life living for the glory of Your name. You have the power to change my heart so that it is accustomed to beating the way Your heart beats.*

*O Lord, I bow my heart before You today and recognize that You alone are worthy of all that I am. You alone deserve my love, my devotion, my worship and all that resides within me.*

*My life is Yours, King Jesus. Teach me how to die to myself so that I might live for Christ. Teach me to treasure You above everything else. Fix my eyes on You, the Author and Perfecter of my faith.*

*May I live today in such a way that my actions stem from my conviction that my life is now hidden in Christ and the life I live in this body I live for the Son of God who loved me and gave Himself for me.*

*I pray these things for Your names sake, Jesus. Amen.*

# DISCIPLESHIP IN PROGRESS
## WHAT DOES ALL THIS LOOK LIKE ANYWAY?

Of course we know we're not all going to have the same experiences with discipleship. It's fair to say we're not all going to approach the task of making disciples the same way. And that truly is something to be celebrated.

As clear as the mandate is for us to make disciples of the nations, it's not as clear *how* we're supposed to go about doing this. When Jesus told us to make disciples by teaching them to obey, He was in essence instructing us to teach them *what* and *how* to obey. Teaching someone what and how to obey is vastly different from simply teaching adherence to a set of rules. Teaching someone factual information about the rules to follow and the pitfalls to avoid is entirely different from what we're describing here. Teaching someone what and how to obey always gets fleshed out in real life relationships. You don't have to look further than Jesus' example with His disciples and Paul's relationships with guys like Timothy and Titus.

I'd like to share with you a few of the ways that I've discipled people over the years. I'd love to be able to tell you that all of these ways are tried and true and all of the people who I've discipled continue to follow hard after Jesus. Neither of those statements are true though.

It pains me to know that some people that I've invested in over the years have wandered away. I'm not sure if they just wandered away from the high cost and significant demands of a discipleship relationship or if they walked away from whatever semblance of faith they once professed. In either case though, most of those who've walked away appear to be living for their own agendas. They've chosen to pursue a life void of the distinguishing hallmarks of someone running hard after the heart of the King.

So, what does this look like anyway? How should we go about investing our lives in this process of discipleship? If we agree that we should indeed change the direction of our lives and begin to take seriously the charge of Jesus to make disciples of the nations, what exactly is that going to look like for us?

Let me share a few of the ways my wife Julie and I have invested in making disciples.

For the past twenty years we've looked for and prayed for people that we can invest in and point to Jesus. Sometimes we went looking for them, sometimes they came looking for us. Both of these approaches seem to have their pro's and con's. I've found though that those who find us tend to be marked by a deeper and more profound hunger for God and desire to follow Jesus. This is not exclusively the case, but more often than not it is.

When we get connected with someone that we believe God wants us to invest in, we usually meet with them at least once a week at a predetermined time and place. Sometimes these meetings last two hours. Sometimes they last six hours. In either case though, we approach these times together with a sense of sobriety and awareness because we just don't want to miss anything that God is planning on doing through our investment with these dear people.

Most of the time we have these discipleship meetings in our home. Julie will have one of the girls over and I'll take our kids out. Or sometimes she'll have her entire D-Group (discipleship group) over. When they all come to the house I usually try to find another place to go. Having seven kids around can distract from what God is intending to do as He speaks to hearts and changes lives. So we remove as many of the distractions as possible. Like I said, we try to approach these discipleship meetings with a sense of sobriety and sensitivity.

Other times we might have our discipleship meetings in parks, in café's or restaurants, at the food court in the mall, etc. There's nothing like sharing a meal with someone. It has the awesome potential to build a sense of intimacy, trust and familiarity. So we try finding a booth or table somewhere out of the way of heavy traffic so we can talk and pray with as little distraction as possible.

There's a fine line here somewhere. Because part of the process of discipleship is modeling real life for those you are discipling. And with that in mind, there are times I want those I'm discipling to see how I treat my wife and kids, raise a family of nine and handle the everyday demands of leading an international ministry. I want to show them how to engage a waiter or waitress in spiritual conversations without appearing as if we're some religious whack-jobs who are disconnected from reality.

In terms of the material we use, we've chosen several different types of studies over the years. Sometimes we study through a workbook, sometimes a book, sometimes we just work through passages or books of the Bible. Whatever we decide to do, we always make our time revolve around teaching them the Word. We aren't just getting together to shoot the breeze or talk about their problems. We are intentionally teaching them the Word of God and the practical steps to living a life of radical and marked obedience.

Certainly, there are times when we do talk about their personal lives, problems, and issues they may be facing. But that is never the focus of Biblical discipleship. Perhaps that's the focus of counseling or friends that you just hang out with for encouragement. For us though, our discipleship relationships have always centered around intentionally teaching the content and application of the Word of God.

I would just caution you about the material you use as you disciple those that God calls you to. Much of what you find in your local Christian bookstore is more antidotal that addresses only felt needs, as opposed to solid Bible studies that tend to focus on deep truths found in Scripture. So be careful what you use and keep in mind that just because it can be found in a Christian bookstore doesn't necessarily mean it is theologically sound and beneficial to use.

Another very valuable approach we've taken is in the form of small groups that we call D-Groups or Life Groups. For high school and college students, these groups are limited to six or seven people and are gender and age specific. By that I mean, groups are comprised of people of the same gender and same approximate age. This lends itself to a deeper level of transparency and vulnerability when working with these students and young adults.

If we're talking about adults in Life Groups, these groups are typically mixed ages and mixed genders. We don't usually put stipulations on these particular groups. Sometimes they are put together geographically so people aren't driving two hours every time the group meets. But by and large these are open groups with little or no demographic criteria.

Whether we are working with individuals or groups, guys or gals, students or adults, we always explain up front what discipleship is all about, what it's going to look like, what it will likely cost them, how long it will last, etc, etc. Our goal in explaining this on the front end is to answer potential objections and address potential obstacles before they arise.

And because this is such a big commitment on both of our parts we also have them sign a covenant. This helps clarify for people up front what exactly the expectations are and what will be required of them. I've included a sample discipleship covenant for you to look at.[1]

With college students, we tend to start the D-groups at the beginning of a semester and take a short break when the semester is finished simply because so many college students vacate the campuses and head home for their breaks. Our goal though is always to have the same group continue meeting after they return from their short holidays.

In an effort to eliminate unnecessary headaches and to avoid wasting valuable man hours, we promote and advertise these D-Groups for several weeks before we actually launch them. And we give ample warning that once the D-Groups start, they are closed to new people. If someone new wants to get involved in a D-Group after they've already started, we ask them to wait until new groups are formed at the beginning of the following semester.

We don't typically add new people to existing D-Groups and we rarely allow students to migrate to other D-Groups. We've worked diligently to guard against the high level of transiency that often marks student discipleship groups. It takes time to build trust, accountability, vulnerability, consistency and transparency (which are all highly critical to building an effective discipleship relationship), so we strive to ensure we're intentionally and consistently building those elements into our D-groups. Otherwise, these discipleship groups will become fluid and our efforts to systematically disciple those whom God has entrusted to us will be substantially weakened.

For adults, we tend to make the groups last indefinitely. Some churches and leaders do them differently. We've found though that if our goal is to make radical, God-honoring, Christ-exalting, Biblically literate, passionate followers of Jesus Christ, that can only be accomplished over time. It simply cannot happen in six or eight weeks. Perhaps some good things can happen in a short six or ten week study, but certainly Jesus had something more significant and long term in mind when He modeled this for us with His disciples.

Another difference between student groups and adult groups is that we do allow adults to invite new people to the groups. And for the purposes of function and learning, we usually put a cap on the maximum number of people that we allow in a group. So, when a group begins growing and reaching that cap, we launch new groups from people in the existing group. Which means there needs to be someone on deck ready, willing and able to effectively launch and lead the new group. We believe individual, spiritual growth will most often times naturally result in corporate, numeric growth. And the byproduct of that consists of continually launching new discipleship groups from existing groups. Keep in mind that the ultimate goal is to make reproducing disciples.

When I first started discipling people, I pursued them pretty hardcore. I called a lot, checked in a lot, and kept pretty tight tabs to be sure they were doing the required work. I had as my goal to ensure they were keeping up with their assignments and jumping through all the right hoops as befits one being discipled. It's not all rigid and academic though. I also wanted to remind them of my concern for them, my love for them, and my availability to them.

Over the past few years though I've taken a different approach. I'd like to think this is because God is changing my heart and growing me in my understanding of Him and His Word. I trust that my sanctification is fleshing out not just in my heart and in my mind but also in how I live my life. If it doesn't flesh out in real life activities, I wonder if there's really been a change.

Today, I certainly make efforts to keep in touch with those I am actively discipling. But not so much for the purpose of checking in to see if they've completed their assignments. Today, it's more along the lines of hearing their hearts in order to better know where they are so I can know how to more effectively pray for them. It also gives me the pulse of whether or not the discipleship investment I'm making appears to be producing any forward momentum.

Part of this different approach comes from my convictions that you just can't make a pig sing. No matter how hard you try, it simply doesn't happen. What you will do though is anger the pig and become frustrated yourself in the process.

Likewise, we can't make people be hungry for God. As much as we want it for them, we just can't want it enough for other people. They must desire it for themselves. People must have their own hunger and thirst after righteousness. And when they do, their actions will follow suit. They will act like hungry people act.

Instead of me having to chase them all over town to find out how they're doing, what's going on with them, or what God is teaching them, they will often be the ones to initiate that. And when they do, I respond. I just don't waste time trying to make people eat who simply aren't hungry. I believe it's just bad stewardship. We only have so much time and so many hours in the day. There seems to be much more kingdom value in investing my hours in people who seem genuinely hungry to learn and grow, as opposed to trying to find people who will listen, hold them down, and force feed them. One is certainly more effective and bears more fruit than the other.

It should be noted that when I talk about my discipleship strategies, these differ significantly from my evangelistic strategies. When we talk evangelism, we're primarily referring to unregenerate people whose hearts have not been made new. These folks have a great need for salvation and are most often times ignorant of Biblical truth. I tend to pursue those relationships pretty hard until the door seems to close. At which point I move on and trust God to bring other seed planters around in His sovereign timing. If the door doesn't close, I feel I have a responsibility to continue tending to this soil.

I like to ask questions, probe people's hearts, and see where God leads the conversations. In any case though, I just wanted to be clear that the strategy I mentioned in the previous paragraphs as it pertains to discipleship is vastly different from the strategy I employ with building relationships with lost people.

While there clearly are a vast number of different ways to go about discipling someone, the point isn't so much how you're going to do it. Just be sure to keep in the forefront of your mind and methodology that the heart of Biblical discipleship rests in properly teaching people *what* and *how* to obey. It's not just the transfer of facts.

So the question before you isn't so much about the method and means of discipling someone. The million dollar question before you now is – *are you going to do it?* Are you going to join the ranks of millions of others who choose to take God seriously and who are willing to abandon American Christianity to invest the whole of their lives following in the footsteps of Jesus? Will you choose to walk away from the comforts and deception of being a loyal fan of Jesus and invest your life as befits one who has joined a relentless band of radical followers willing to lay down their lives for the sake of His name among the nations?

I hope you'll join the remnant of others who have decided that Jesus is indeed worth living for and dying for.

## OUR PRAYER

*Thank You, Jesus, for the model You set before us in making disciples. The truth is, this endeavor will certainly cost me my life. I recognize that I simply cannot continue to embrace the treasures of this world while being radically obedient to You.*

*I confess I have no idea what to do from here. I'm convinced You have called me to take the gospel to the ends of the earth and to make disciples of all the nations. But where do I start? What's my next step?*

*As Paul prayed for the Ephesians, so I pray for myself that You would give me a spirit of wisdom and revelation so that I might know You better. You alone are the answer to my questions.*

*Bring people to my mind. Help me to know clearly what You're saying and what I need to do to respond appropriately to You. Wasting another day is not an option. I am compelled to move forward in becoming a disciple and making other disciples.*

*Thank You for Your desire to use me. I know I will fail. Certainly I will falter along the way. There will be days when my motives are challenged. I am expecting there to be times when my flesh seems hungrier than my desire for righteousness.*

*Consume me Lord Jesus! I have seen You in the sanctuary and beheld Your power and Your glory. And because Your love is better than life, my lips will praise You. I will praise You as long as I live and in Your name I will lift up my hands. My soul will be satisfied as with the richest of foods.*

*Make me like a tree planted by streams of water, that yields fruit in season. Teach me how to delight myself in You and in Your Word. As I learn how to meditate on it day and night, speak to my heart and reveal Yourself to me. Mark me today, King Jesus. I submit to Your rightful authority.*

*I pray this with a genuine and humble desire that my life would be counted worthy of the high cost of my calling to follow You. Amen.*

# 10

# THE FINAL CHAPTER

## IT HELPS KNOWING HOW IT ALL ENDS

We know God will be victorious. We live with confidence that when God accomplishes His sovereign purposes on earth, the end will come. And when the end comes, it will be an end to life as we know it. As this world comes to an end, God will usher in the age to come and we will spend eternity enjoying the beauty and glory that is God. Until the end comes though, we continue to exhaust our lives and our resources delivering the gospel to the remote corners of the earth and making authentic, radical, selfless, zealous, committed, passionate followers of Jesus Christ. Why? Because He needs us? Absolutely not. We choose to join Him because He loves us, we love Him, and because He has commanded us to.

We also know from reading Scripture that God's chosen instrument to reach the world is His bride - the church of Jesus Christ. He established His church two thousand years ago, ordained it, and sent it on mission to deliver the gospel – the *euangelion* or 'good news' to the ends of the earth. It is precisely this good news that men and women have willingly lost their lives to proclaim. The good news is not simply that one can escape the flames of hell in eternal destruction. The good news is that the glory of God has been revealed in Jesus and that He has invited us and enabled us to make much of His glory among the nations. That is indeed good news!

It is the church, the *ekklesia*, that He's chosen to use to bring the message of salvation to every people and tribe and tongue and language. It is the church that God has chosen to use as the catalyst to make disciples of all the nations. It is the church that God has chosen to use to deliver the message that there is Someone worth living for and worth dying for who stands before all of creation with the simple message to come and die.

And by the church I mean believers. Those who've chosen to align themselves with Jesus Christ. Those who have embraced His truth and obeyed His mission. We are the church. Although God could have devised a trillion different ways to take the gospel to the world and make disciples of the nations, He has chosen to use us.

The mission of God *will be* accomplished. To a large degree though, it rests on our obedience to the great call of God on our lives. That's not to say we can foil God's plans should we choose to opt out. We can't.[1] God *will* accomplish His salvific and redemptive purposes with all people, in all places, in all of time and for all of eternity. We can build our lives and our ministries on this great truth.

The question isn't so much what will God do if we all back out. The real question is, since we know God has promised to complete His work and He desires to use us in that process, *will we jump on board with Him and invest the whole of our lives in delivering the gospel to the ends of the earth and making disciples of all the nations?* That's the real question. The question isn't will He. The real question is will I.

We have the promise from Jesus Himself that He will build His church, and nothing will stop Him. Disease won't stop Him. Famine won't stop Him. War won't stop Him. Apathy and complacency won't stop Him. Nothing in all of creation can halt God's sovereign plan to make His name great among the nations.[2] Nothing. Demons won't stop Him. Pagan worship won't stop Him. Wolves dressed like sheep won't stop Him. Nothing can or will hinder God from accomplishing His purposes. Nothing. Not even hell itself.[3]

There's a remarkable passage in Revelation 5 that reaffirms the worth of Jesus and gives promise that His blood was effective in ransoming people from every tribe and people and language.

"And they sang a new song, saying,
'Worthy are You to take the scroll
and to open its seals, for You were slain,
and by Your blood You ransomed people
for God from every tribe and language
and people and nation,
and You have made them a kingdom
and priests to our God,
and they shall reign on the earth.'"[4]

The work has been done. The salvific purposes of God have been instituted. We don't know who the people are that Jesus ransomed for God, but we know His work on the cross completed the transaction. The purchase has been made. The remaining work belongs to us in delivering the message that will allow them to respond to the gospel and take their designated place as worshippers around the throne of God.

There are men and women, boys and girls, and families scattered across every continent on the globe who are just waiting to hear about this Jesus. They have wasted so much of their lives chasing frivolous dreams that fade into distant yesterdays. These boys, these girls, these old men and women, these moms and dads, they are waiting for us. They don't know they're waiting for us, but they are. They're waiting for us because we have the news that can set them free from the worthless worship of other gods. We have the truth that has the power and the potential to set their hearts aflame for a cause that they can give the whole of their lives to.

But time is running out. The return of Christ is imminent. We know He will come. And we know He will come soon. We don't have the luxury of waiting until we feel called or until we're more prepared. If you're a follower of Jesus Christ rest assured that you have been called and you are prepared. It's time to exhaust the rest of this life that you have on the kingdom of God.

We know that before the end comes, God's work will be accomplished. God is not frantically scrambling for Plan B because some posing Christians backed out or walked away or decided this wasn't for them. The astonishing part is that God is choosing to accomplish His eternal purposes and plans while sovereignly using those of us who will say, "Here I am Lord, send me."

We have been given an opportunity to trade in our lives for the lives God created us for. We have been afforded a grand occasion to embrace Someone and something worth living for and Someone and something worth dying for. We would do well to recognize the world in which we live is filled with billions of people who still need to hear the gospel and billions of people who have not yet been invited to join in the anthem of heaven by expending their lives for the sake of His name among the nations. Many are simply waiting to hear about such a cause.

As radical followers of Jesus Christ, we have been called and commissioned to invest the totality of our lives in delivering the gospel to the far corners of the earth and to make disciples of all the nations. This we know for certain.

We have a great call on our lives and the One who is doing the bidding is worthy of all that we have and all that we are. At the end of the day it simply comes down to this – will you rise to the occasion and invest your remaining days and your remaining dollars in making much of His name among the nations. As for me….

**I will be. I will make. I will go. I will give. I will speak. I will obey. I will trust. I will exalt. I will cherish. I will labor. I will magnify. I will glorify. I will choose. I will forsake. I will……..**

**Will you?**

# ACKNOWLEDGEMENTS

This book has been a work in progress for many years. My heart beats for Biblical discipleship and I long for others to see with clarity the same call of Jesus I see throughout the pages of Scripture.

It all started with five guys who invested in my life when I first made the decision to follow hard after Jesus. Dave Tulka, Bob Bray, Bruce Hodge, Bill Keith and Michael Holt – I am forever indebted for the risk you took over twenty years ago in helping me understand the beauty of embracing the gospel and unapologetically laying down my own desires in pursuit of living out His.

I am also grateful to Dr. Jack Graham and Dr. Keith Thomas for faithfully preaching and teaching the Word of Life each week during their time at First Baptist Church of West Palm Beach. You labored in your study so your delivery in the pulpit would be clear. And it was! Your teaching left an indelible mark on my own desire to be faithful to the heart of God as I learn to rightly divide Scripture and teach it around the world.

I owe much to Josh McDowell. Thank you, Josh, for investing in my life and allowing me to watch and learn from your example. My time with you is always profitable beyond measure. I count it an honor to call you a friend and am humbled that you call me one. Let's do Baja again soon!

My friend, Barry St. Clair, has been a great source of wisdom and encouragement over the years. Thank you, Barry, for walking away from the allures of American Christianity and faithfully modeling a life devoted to making disciples who will faithfully make other disciples.

Thank you to my pastor and dear friend, Steve Harris. Your friendship over the years and your wise counsel are both invaluable to me. It is a privilege and honor for me to partner with you in ministry. Thanks for encouraging me in the work that God has called me to. I look forward to celebrating together the work that God will do as we continue to invest our lives in making disciples and exhaust our resources in making His name great to all those scattered around the globe.

Thank you to Don Newman and Karla Castellon, my new friends at Xulon publishing. Your guidance and expertise have been a valuable asset as I've embarked on this wild adventure of writing my first book.

I am grateful to Kathy Knight for taking a red pen to my original manuscript. Thank you, Kathy, for your helpful suggestions and your guidance to help ensure that what I've written turns out to be somewhat understandable.

Thank you to Susie Hepler and my family at North Asheville Christian School for the privilege of allowing me to walk with you through the process of discipling your students. This initial season of trial and error will soon reap the blessing of discipleship being a part of NACS's DNA. God will use your commitment and investment to make His name great among the nations. NACS will someday be a model for how Christian schools all across the country can effectively make Biblical and radical disciples of their students. Don't give up! *"Endure hardship like a good soldier....no one serving as a soldier gets involved in civilian affairs...he wants to please his commanding officer. Similarly, we only receive the victors crown if we compete according to the rules. The hardworking farmer should be the first to share in the crops. Reflect on what I'm saying, for the Lord will give you insight into all this."*

Thank you, Tom Birk. I know you trekked half way across the country so we could hang out together, only to discover our time hanging out would consist of you watching me write and edit this book. Thanks for your great suggestions for chapter six. It's truly an honor to be able to watch you go for broke! And I look forward to how God will use our friendship over the years to come.

I could not be more grateful to my oldest son, Dawson. Thank you, Doogie, for all the time you spent developing creative ideas for the logo and cover for my first book. I hope this is the start of a life-long partnership in ministry. Nothing would bring me more joy.

It is an honor and joy to be called "daddy" by seven amazing kids. Thank you, Dawson, Ezekiel, Cassie, Nana, Moses, Sydney, and Ephraim for making the needed sacrifices so daddy could work on this project. I'll make it up to you soon. Anyone up for pulling an all-nighter and sneaking down to Krispy Kreme? Mommy will never know we left.

I owe a huge thank you to my wife Julie for reading my manuscripts along the way. Your wise and gentle suggestions reflect your wise and gentle heart. Thanks for laboring through this project alongside of me and picking up all the extra work around the house while I finished this project. I owe you big time! And look honey, I even used a capital B in all the right places!

Finally and most importantly - there is no way to properly say Thank You to Jesus, my Redeemer, Counselor, Physician, Friend, Mediator, High Priest, King, Lord, Master, Intercessor, and so many other amazing and indescribable things. I'm keenly aware of my deep need for You to envelop my heart and provide victory over the wicked passions and desires that tend to reside in the crevices of my soul. Please continue to capture my attention and my affections, and bring into submission every thought of mine so that they will all be obedient to You. Jesus, Your radical grace to me is not without affect. You are my life, my breath, the reason I am still alive. Thank You for Your irresistible grace, Your audacious mercy, and Your indescribable worth. As You continue to enlarge my heart and as I run in the way of Your commands, please use my efforts in this project to make Your name great among the nations.

# NOTES

## INTRODUCTION

1. Here are a few books about discipleship. Dirk Helmling is not necessarily endorsing any of the titles listed. *The Disciple-Making Church*, Bill Hull; *Mere Discipleship*, Lee Camp; *Transforming Discipleship*, Greg Ogden; *The Complete Book of Discipleship*, Bill Hull; *The Great Omission*, Dallas Willard; *The Master Plan of Discipleship*, Robert Coleman; *After McDonaldization*, John Drane; *Personal Disciplemaking*, Christopher Adsit; *The Cost of Discipleship*, Dietrich Bonhoeffer; *Breaking the Discipleship Code*, David Putnam; *Spiritual Discipleship*, J. Oswald Sanders.

## CHAPTER I – A BARREN LANDSCAPE

1. I recently heard a pastor explain why he wears jeans on Sundays. He responded by saying...."I wear jeans on Sundays because this is the way I dress every day of the week. And I believe God wants me to be the same person Monday, Tuesday, Wednesday, Thursday, Friday, Saturday, Sunday. And I want to make a point about that. My heart should be right all throughout the week and I should be the same person when I leave this room as when I come into this room." Francis Chan – *Is it wrong to wear jeans?* Youtube.com

2. 1 Samuel 16.7 "But the Lord said to Samuel, 'Do not look on his appearance or on the height of his stature, because I have rejected him. For the Lord sees not as man sees: man looks on the outward appearance, but the Lord looks on the heart.'"

3. Revelation 3.14-22 "And to the angel of the church in Laodicea write: 'The words of the Amen, the faithful and true witness, the beginning of God's creation. 'I know your works: you are neither cold nor hot. Would that you were either cold or hot! So, because you are lukewarm, and neither hot nor cold, I will spit you out of My mouth. For you say, I am rich, I have prospered, and I need nothing, not realizing that you are wretched, pitiable, poor, blind, and naked. I counsel you to buy from Me gold refined by fire, so that you may be rich, and white garments so that you may clothe yourself and the shame of your nakedness may not be seen, and salve to anoint your eyes, so that you may see. Those whom I love, I reprove and discipline, so be zealous and repent. Behold, I stand at the door and knock. If anyone hears My voice and opens the door, I will come in to him and eat with him, and he with Me. The one who conquers, I will grant him to sit

with Me on My throne, as I also conquered and sat down with My Father on His throne. He who has an ear, let him hear what the Spirit says to the churches.'"

4.    Lakewood Church: www.lakewood.cc

5.    Joel Osteen, *Your Best Life Now for Moms; Starting Your Best Life Now. A Guide for New Adventures and Stages on Your Journey; Your Best Life Begins Each Morning: Devotions to Start Every New Day of the Year; Become a Better You; It's Your Time; Your Best Life Now: 7 Steps to Living at Your Full Potential; It's Your Time: Activate Your Faith, Achieve Your Dreams, and Increase in God's Favor.*

6.    1 Timothy 1.3-7 "As I urged you when I was going to Macedonia, remain at Ephesus so that you may charge certain persons not to teach any different doctrine, nor to devote themselves to myths and endless genealogies, which promote speculations rather than the stewardship from God that is by faith. The aim of our charge is love that issues from a pure heart and a good conscience and a sincere faith. Certain persons, by swerving from these, have wandered away into vain discussion, desiring to be teachers of the law, without understanding either what they are saying or the things about which they make confident assertions."

7.    This interview with Bill Hybels can be found at www.outofur.com. Look for *Willow Creek Repents?* October 18, 2007.

8.    Isaiah 26.8 (NIV)

# CHAPTER 2 - THE CYCLE OF INSANITY

1.    John 6.60-71 "When many of His disciples heard it, they said, 'This is a hard saying; who can listen to it?' But Jesus, knowing in Himself that His disciples were grumbling about this, said to them, 'Do you take offense at this? Then what if you were to see the Son of Man ascending to where He was before? It is the Spirit who gives life; the flesh is no help at all. The words that I have spoken to you are spirit and life. But there are some of you who do not believe.' (For Jesus knew from the beginning who those were who did not believe, and who it was who would betray Him.) And He said, 'This is why I told you that no one can come to Me unless it is granted him by the Father.' After this many of His disciples turned back and no longer walked with Him. So Jesus said to the Twelve, 'Do you want to go away as well?' Simon Peter answered Him, 'Lord, to whom shall we go? You have the words of eternal life, and we have believed, and have come to know, that You are the Holy One of God.' Jesus answered them, 'Did I not choose

you, the Twelve? And yet one of you is a devil.' He spoke of Judas the son of Simon Iscariot, for he, one of the Twelve, was going to betray Him."

2.  Josh McDowell – www.josh.org
3.  Matthew 7.22-23 (NIV)
4.  Proverbs 26.11

# CHAPTER 3 - WILL THE REAL JESUS PLEASE STAND

1.  Bill Hull, *The Complete Book of Discipleship*
2.  John 10.30; John 14.7; John 6.40; John 14.6
3.  Dietrich Bonhoeffer, *The Cost of Discipleship*
4.  John 21.25
5.  Hebrews 4.15 "For we do not have a High Priest who is unable to sympathize with our weaknesses, but One who in every respect has been tempted as we are, yet without sin."

# CHAPTER 4 – A DIVISIVE LINE IN THE SAND

1.  www.culteducation.com
2.  Helpful cult resources:
    a.  Dean C. Halverson: *The Compact Guide To World Religions*
    b.  Josh McDowell: *New Evidence That Demands A Verdict*
    c.  Josh McDowell and Don Stewart: *Handbook of Today's Religions*
    d.  Norman Geisler: *Christian Apologetics*
    e.  Lee Strobel: *The Case for Christ*
    f.  Lee Strobel: *The Case for Faith*
    g.  Walter Martin: *The Kingdom of the Cults*
3.  Characteristics of a cult:
    a.  Does it attempt to attack or change the person, work or deity of Christ?
    b.  Is salvation by a new, unique, non-Scriptural method, works, or something other than faith in Jesus and His work on the cross?
    c.  Is membership with this group required for salvation?
    d.  Is the Doctrine of the Trinity compromised?
    e.  Does it attempt to change the teaching about the person, Deity, and/or work of the Holy Spirit?
    f.  Is the Holy Spirit credited with revealing things that are contrary to what He has already revealed in the Bible?
    g.  Is God being made to seem more like man?
    h.  Is man being made to seem more like God?

i.  Is someone or something being presented as an authority equal to or superior to the Bible?

j.  Is the teaching or interpretation of one person or select group of people seen as the only acceptable material or guide by which you are to study the Bible?

k.  Does it edify the Church and build up the body of Christ, or does it seek to give glory to a person or organization?

l.  Are claims and/or prophecies made that cannot be substantiated or that have failed to come about?

m.  Are terms commonly used in "Christianity" redefined and given new "non-Biblical" meanings?

n.  Is the teaching or activity consistent with the New Testament?

o.  Is this a matter of tradition, culture and emotions; or is it Bible?

p.  Does this group or teaching force interpretations of Scripture passages that make the Bible contradict itself?

q.  Does the movement or group produce healthy, well-balanced, growing disciples?

r.  Is the teaching, movement, or group focused on the entire message of the gospel of Jesus Christ, or are they focused only on a few specific issues? For example: end-time prophecy, deliverance ministry, healing campaigns, prosperity teachings, etc.

4.  Matthew 5.11-13 "Blessed are you when others revile you and persecute you and utter all kinds of evil against you falsely on My account. Rejoice and be glad, for your reward is great in heaven, for so they persecuted the prophets who were before you."

5.  Matthew 7.21-23

6.  Matthew 10.16-18

7.  Matthew 10.22

8.  Matthew 25.31-46 "When the Son of Man comes in His glory, and all the angels with Him, then He will sit on His glorious throne. Before Him will be gathered all the nations, and He will separate people one from another as a shepherd separates the sheep from the goats. And He will place the sheep on His right, but the goats on the left. Then the King will say to those on His right, 'Come, you who are blessed by My Father, inherit the kingdom prepared for you from the foundation of the world. For I was hungry and you gave Me food, I was thirsty and you gave Me drink, I was a stranger and you welcomed Me, I was naked and you clothed Me, I was sick and you visited Me, I was in prison and you came to Me.' Then the righteous will answer Him, saying, 'Lord, when did we see You hungry and

feed You, or thirsty and give You drink? And when did we see You a stranger and welcome You, or naked and clothe You? And when did we see You sick or in prison and visit You?' And the King will answer them, 'Truly, I say to you, as you did it to one of the least of these My brothers, you did it to Me.' Then He will say to those on His left, 'Depart from Me, you cursed, into the eternal fire prepared for the devil and his angels. For I was hungry and you gave Me no food, I was thirsty and you gave Me no drink, I was a stranger and you did not welcome Me, naked and you did not clothe Me, sick and in prison and you did not visit Me.' Then they also will answer, saying, 'Lord, when did we see You hungry or thirsty or a stranger or naked or sick or in prison, and did not minister to You?' Then He will answer them, saying, 'Truly, I say to you, as you did not do it to one of the least of these, you did not do it to Me.' And these will go away into eternal punishment, but the righteous into eternal life."

9.  Mark 4.1-20 "Again He began to teach beside the sea. And a very large crowd gathered about Him, so that He got into a boat and sat in it on the sea, and the whole crowd was beside the sea on the land. And He was teaching them many things in parables, and in His teaching he said to them: 'Listen! A sower went out to sow. And as he sowed, some seed fell along the path, and the birds came and devoured it. Other seed fell on rocky ground, where it did not have much soil, and immediately it sprang up, since it had no depth of soil. And when the sun rose, it was scorched, and since it had no root, it withered away. Other seed fell among thorns, and the thorns grew up and choked it, and it yielded no grain. And other seeds fell into good soil and produced grain, growing up and increasing and yielding thirtyfold and sixtyfold and a hundredfold.' And He said, 'He who has ears to hear, let him hear.' And when He was alone, those around Him with the twelve asked Him about the parables. And He said to them, 'To you has been given the secret of the kingdom of God, but for those outside everything is in parables, so that they may indeed see but not perceive, and may indeed hear but not understand, lest they should turn and be forgiven.' And He said to them, 'Do you not understand this parable? How then will you understand all the parables? The sower sows the Word. And these are the ones along the path, where the Word is sown: when they hear, Satan immediately comes and takes away the Word that is sown in them. And these are the ones sown on rocky ground: the ones who, when they hear the Word, immediately receive it with joy. And they have no root in themselves, but endure for a while; then, when tribulation or persecution arises on account of the Word, immediately they fall away. And others are the ones sown among thorns. They are those who hear the

Word, but the cares of the world and the deceitfulness of riches and the desires for other things enter in and choke the Word, and it proves unfruitful. But those that were sown on the good soil are the ones who hear the Word and accept it and bear fruit, thirtyfold and sixtyfold and a hundredfold.'"

10. Matthew 6.24 "No one can serve two masters, for either he will hate the one and love the other, or he will be devoted to the one and despise the other. You cannot serve God and money."

11. Mark 12.41-44 "And He sat down opposite the treasury and watched the people putting money into the offering box. Many rich people put in large sums. And a poor widow came and put in two small copper coins, which make a penny. And He called His disciples to Him and said to them, 'Truly, I say to you, this poor widow has put in more than all those who are contributing to the offering box. For they all contributed out of their abundance, but she out of her poverty has put in everything she had, all she had to live on.'"

12. Matthew 19.24 "Again I tell you, it is easier for a camel to go through the eye of a needle than for a rich person to enter the kingdom of God."

13. Matthew 25.31-46 "When the Son of Man comes in His glory, and all the angels with Him, then He will sit on His glorious throne. Before Him will be gathered all the nations, and He will separate people one from another as a shepherd separates the sheep from the goats. And He will place the sheep on His right, but the goats on the left. Then the King will say to those on His right, 'Come, you who are blessed by My Father, inherit the kingdom prepared for you from the foundation of the world. For I was hungry and you gave Me food, I was thirsty and you gave Me drink, I was a stranger and you welcomed Me, I was naked and you clothed Me, I was sick and you visited Me, I was in prison and you came to Me.' Then the righteous will answer Him, saying, 'Lord, when did we see You hungry and feed You, or thirsty and give You drink? And when did we see You a stranger and welcome You, or naked and clothe You? And when did we see You sick or in prison and visit You?' And the King will answer them, 'Truly, I say to you, as you did it to one of the least of these My brothers, you did it to Me.' Then He will say to those on His left, 'Depart from Me, you cursed, into the eternal fire prepared for the devil and his angels. For I was hungry and you gave Me no food, I was thirsty and you gave Me no drink, I was a stranger and you did not welcome Me, naked and you did not clothe Me, sick and in prison and you did not visit Me.' Then they also will answer, saying, 'Lord, when did we see You hungry or thirsty or a stranger or naked or sick or in prison, and did not minister to You?' Then

He will answer them, saying, 'Truly, I say to you, as you did not do it to one of the least of these, you did not do it to Me.' And these will go away into eternal punishment, but the righteous into eternal life."

14. 1 Timothy 6.10 "For the love of money is a root of all kinds of evils. It is through this craving that some have wandered away from the faith and pierced themselves with many pangs."

15. Matthew 19.21 "Jesus said to him, 'If you would be perfect, go, sell what you possess and give to the poor, and you will have treasure in heaven; and come, follow Me.'"

16. Matthew 8.20 "And Jesus said to him, 'Foxes have holes, and birds of the air have nests, but the Son of Man has nowhere to lay his head.'"

17. John MacArthur - www.gty.org/blog/B091207

18. YouTube - John Piper and the Prosperity Gospel, http://www.youtube.com/watch?v=PTc_FoELt8s

19. YouTube - Joel Osteen and the gospel, http://www.youtube.com/watch?v=pKF_QgNezBY

20. We should note that there are some beliefs common to nearly all forms of Hinduism that can be identified, and these basic beliefs are generally regarded as boundaries outside of which lies either heresy or non-Hindu religion. These fundamental Hindu beliefs include: the authority of the Vedas (the oldest Indian sacred texts) and the Brahmans (priests); the existence of an enduring soul that transmigrates from one body to another at death (reincarnation); and the law of karma that determines one's destiny both in this life and the next. Note that a specific belief about God or gods is not considered one of the essentials, which is a major difference between Hinduism and strictly monotheistic religions like Christianity, Judaism, Islam and Sikhism. Most Hindus are devoted followers of one of the principal gods Shiva, Vishnu or Shakti, and often others besides, yet all these are regarded as manifestations of a single Reality. The ultimate goal of all Hindus is release (*moksha*) from the cycle of rebirth (*samsara*). For those of a devotional bent, this means being in God's presence, while those of a philosophical persuasion look forward to uniting with God as a drop of rain merges with the sea.

21. 1 Timothy 2.5 "For there is one God, and there is one Mediator between God and men, the man Christ Jesus."

22. Matthew 16.25 "For whoever would save his life will lose it, but whoever loses his life for My sake will find it."

23. John 14.22-24 "Judas (not Iscariot) said to Him, 'Lord, how is it that You will manifest Yourself to us, and not to the world?' Jesus answered him, 'If anyone loves Me, he will keep My Word, and My Father will love him, and We will come to him and make Our home with him. Whoever does not love Me does not keep My Words. And the Word that you hear is not Mine but the Father's who sent Me.'"

# CHAPTER 5 - NO MORE PATTY CAKE

1.  Psalm 66.18 "If I had cherished sin in my heart, the Lord would not have listened." (NIV)
2.  Malachi 1.11 "'My name will be great among the nations, from where the sun rises to where it sets. In every place incense and pure offerings will be brought to Me, because My name will be great among the nations,' says the LORD Almighty." (NIV)

# CHAPTER 6 - GOING FOR BROKE

1.  1 Peter 4.12
2.  1 Peter 2.12; 3.1; 3.13-17
    *Read the entire book of 1 Peter. It helps shine a light on God's sovereignty in the face of suffering.
3.  Philippians 1.19-21

# CHAPTER 7 - THE MULTIPLICATION BLUEPRINT

1.  Matthew 28.16-20 "Now the eleven disciples went to Galilee, to the mountain to which Jesus had directed them. And when they saw Him they worshiped Him, but some doubted. And Jesus came and said to them, 'All authority in heaven and on earth has been given to Me. Go therefore and make disciples of all nations, baptizing them in the name of the Father and of the Son and of the Holy Spirit, teaching them to observe all that I have commanded you. And behold, I am with you always, to the end of the age.'"
2.  2 Timothy 4.3-4 "For the time is coming when people will not endure sound teaching, but having itching ears they will accumulate for themselves teachers to suit their own passions, and will turn away from listening to the truth and wander off into myths."
3.  John 14.23-24

# CHAPTER 8 - DISCIPLE MAKING 101

1.  Psalm 119.18
    Ephesians 1.15-20 "I do not cease to give thanks for you, remembering you in my prayers, that the God of our Lord Jesus Christ, the Father of glory, may give you a spirit of wisdom and of revelation in the knowledge of Him, having the eyes of your hearts enlightened, that you may know what is the hope to which He has called you, what are the riches of His glorious

inheritance in the saints, and what is the immeasurable greatness of His power toward us who believe, according to the working of His great might that He worked in Christ when He raised Him from the dead and seated Him at His right hand in the heavenly places."

2.  Matthew 13.18-19 "Hear then the parable of the sower: When anyone hears the word of the kingdom and does not understand it, the evil one comes and snatches away what has been sown in his heart. This is what was sown along the path."

    Isaiah 42.24-25 "Who gave up Jacob to the looter, and Israel to the plunderers? Was it not the LORD, against whom we have sinned, in whose ways they would not walk, and whose law they would not obey? So He poured on him the heat of His anger and the might of battle; it set him on fire all around, but he did not understand; it burned him up, but he did not take it to heart."

    Psalm 53.2-3 "God looks down from heaven on the children of man to see if there are any who understand, who seek after God."

    Psalm 119.27 "Make me understand the way of Your precepts, and I will meditate on Your wondrous works."

    Psalm 119.34 "Give me understanding, that I may keep Your law and observe it with my whole heart."

    Psalm 119.73 "Your hands have made and fashioned me; give me understanding that I may learn Your commandments."

    Psalm 119.144 "Your testimonies are righteous forever; give me understanding that I may live."

3.  Matthew 13.19-23 "When anyone hears the Word of the kingdom and does not understand it, the evil one comes and snatches away what has been sown in his heart. This is what was sown along the path. As for what was sown on rocky ground, this is the one who hears the Word and immediately receives it with joy, yet he has no root in himself, but endures for a while, and when tribulation or persecution arises on account of the Word, immediately he falls away. As for what was sown among thorns, this is the one who hears the Word, but the cares of the world and the deceitfulness of riches choke the Word, and it proves unfruitful. As for what was sown on good soil, this is the one who hears the Word and understands it. He indeed bears fruit and yields, in one case a hundredfold, in another sixty, and in another thirty."

4.  Bill Hull, *The Complete Book of Discipleship*

5.  James 2.19 "You believe that God is one; you do well. Even the demons believe—and shudder!"

6.  Bill Hull, *The Complete Book of Discipleship*

7. John 14.23; 1 John 5.3 (NIV)
8. Matthew 28.20

# CHAPTER 9 - DISCIPLESHIP IN PROGRESS

1. A sample discipleship covenant

---

## A Disciples Covenant

*In order to grow to be a passionate disciple of Jesus Christ who will
be committed to investing my life in making other disciples,
I commit myself to the following expectations:*

I will complete all assignments on a weekly basis prior to my
discipleship meetings in order to maximize this time together.

I will meet weekly with my discipleship partner for at least two hours
in a concerted effort to be taught the Word of God and to
pray together.

I will offer myself fully to this discipleship process with the
anticipation that I am entering a time of accelerated
transformation during this discipleship period.

I will contribute to a climate of honesty, trust, and vulnerability as I
commit myself to personal growth and maturity with my
discipleship partner.

I will continue the discipleship mandate by committing myself to
invest the rest of my life in learning to be a passionate and
obedient disciple of Jesus Christ.

As God gives me opportunities, I will commit my time and resources
in making other disciples.

Signed (discipler)_____

Signed (disciplee)_____

Date _____

---

# CHAPTER 10 - THE FINAL CHAPTER

1. Job 42.2; Isaiah 14.27; Ephesians 1.11
2. Malachi 1.11 "For from the rising of the sun to its setting My name will be
   great among the nations, and in every place incense will be offered to My

name, and a pure offering. For My name will be great among the nations, says the LORD of hosts."

3.    Matthew 16.18 "And I tell you that you are Peter, and on this rock I will build My church, and the gates of Hades will not overcome it."

4.    Revelation 5.9-10

# ABOUT THE AUTHOR

Dirk Helmling has been married to his best friend, Julie, for over eighteen years. They currently have seven children – three biological kids and four kids they've adopted from Liberia, Africa. The Helmling's make their home in the mountains of Western North Carolina.

Dirk's been on numerous church staff teams around the country. His first love in ministry is teaching God's Word and helping people understand that the cause of Christ, though costly, is worth living for and worth dying for.

Dirks own call and response to Jesus takes him across the United States and around the world, teaching God's Word. He also spends considerable time training pastors overseas and leads small teams on international mission trips several times a year.

Although Dirk loves to teach God's Word to people around the world, he understands his primary call is to teach his own children how to discover all that God is in Christ to the world. Dirk and Julie are training their kids to love God more than they love anything else with the hope that they will one day abandon their lives to make His name great among the nations.

Dirk is currently working on writing his second book (about parenting!) which will be available soon. Check the 29.11 Ministries website for updates on Dirk's latest project.

To find out more about Dirk Helmling and 29.11 Ministries, go to **www.2911.org**.

# ABOUT 29.11 MINISTRIES

29.11 has several facets of ministry they focus their time and resources on - Dirks writing and speaking engagements, discipleship training and ministry equipping for pastors and youth pastors nationally and internationally, and orphan care ministry and sustainable projects in Africa.

If you would like to book Dirk for a speaking engagement or you're interested in finding out more about 29.11 Ministries, please visit our website at **www.2911.org**.

If you would like to order multiple copies of *The Cost Of The Disconnect,* please contact the 29.11 Ministries office directly for bulk discounts.

**THE COST OF THE DISCONNECT**
29.11 Ministries
69 Briarwood Road
Asheville, NC  28804
www.2911.org
828.691.2911